The Science
of
MARKETING *by* MAIL
by
HOMER J. BUCKLEY

PRESIDENT *of the* NATIONALLY KNOWN FIRM
of
BUCKLEY, DEMENT & COMPANY
CHICAGO

✿

ORGANIZER *and* FIRST PRESIDENT
DIRECT MAIL ADVERTISING ASSOCIATION

✿

CHAIRMAN, MARKETING COMMISSION
Y. M. C. A. SCHOOLS, CHICAGO

✿

STAFF LECTURER
CLEVELAND SCHOOL *of* ADVERTISING
UNIVERSITY OF WISCONSIN
SCHOOL OF COMMERCE

B. C. FORBES PUBLISHING COMPANY
120 FIFTH AVENUE, NEW YORK CITY

TABLE OF CONTENTS

PAGE

I

THE EVOLUTION OF MARKETING METHODS......   1

Time for distributors to wake up — Practical proof of the economy of mail merchandising — Development of trading methods — The benefits of a common language — Buying follows desire — Development of long distance markets — Larger sales and their effect on production costs — The fundamentals of direct selling defined.

II

MAIL SELLING PLANS BASED ON STATISTICS.....   22

The importance of facts and figures in every business — Costs are the keynote to success — How selling costs are determined — How volume of orders is predetermined — How the appropriation for selling by mail is determined.

III

THE ECONOMIC VALUE OF TRUTH IN MARKETING BY MAIL...................................   46

Distrust and suspicion, major sales resistances — Confidence in the customer a demonstrated success — Persistence in mail selling necessary to bring results — Goodwill promoters must be truthful.

IV

USING THE MAILS TO MAKE SALES.............   56
The mail order business — its merits and limitations — Mail order methods that have won
— Comparison of retail and mail order selling
— How dealers are sold large shipments of
merchandise through the mail — How dealer
business is held and stimulated by mail efforts.

V

MANUFACTURERS WHO HAVE BECOME MERCHANTS
    BY MAIL SELLING......................   83
Selling problem vitally important to every
manufacturer — Solving the problem of the
manufacturer who has a good product — How
to locate live dealers — How dealers are kept
on their toes — How the goodwill of dealers
stimulates sales.

VI

OPENING NEW TERRITORY AND INCREASING SALES
    FOR JOBBERS AND RETAILERS...........   103
How the stimulus of the sales call changes indifference to enthusiasm — Retailers sell in
rural districts by using mail selling methods —
How retailers welcome the coöperation of wholesalers and manufacturers — The basis of dealer
coöperation.

VII

HOW THE MAILS ARE USED TO STRENGTHEN THE
    HANDS OF THE SALES FORCE.............   127
The high cost of sending salesmen on cold leads

— Increased percentage of sales where missionary work has been accomplished through the mail — The economic folly of using a "closer" for educative work — "Pepping" up the sales force with new ideas — Building goodwill for salesmen.

VIII

BUILDING THE PRESTIGE OF AN INSTITUTION BY MAIL 154
Sales dependent on individuality have hazardous permanent value — The unstable position of the wholesaler who pushes another's trademark exclusively — The insecurity of the manufacturer who sells all of his products to a few concerns — The dependability of the volume of business produced by selling the institution by mail.

IX

FINANCING A MAIL SELLING CAMPAIGN 177
Appropriating a portion of selling cost to pay for mail selling — How an advertising budget is made up to include mail selling — Definite appropriations should be decided on — Proportion of mail and national advertising used by large merchandisers.

X

REGULATING THE MARKET BY MAIL 197
Value and sources of market information — Counteracting business slumps — Preparing campaigns to overcome depression — Broad-

casting price changes without competitors'
knowledge — Maintaining prices by sending
out goodwill messengers — Using the mails to
humanize failure to give service.

XI

ORGANIZED KNOWLEDGE IN MAIL SELLING 222
Need for analytical minds — The place of good
copy and illustrations — The place for mechani-
cal skill and specialized knowledge — The need
for accurate postal information.

XII

THE CASH VALUE OF MAILING LISTS........... 244
Mortality of different lists — Sub-dividing lists
and a master list — Building mailing lists —
How reputable list houses anticipate your needs.

XIII

THE RELATION OF PUBLICITY TO SELLING BY MAIL 263
Co-ordination of general and dealer advertising
— Importance of deciding policy — Where
trade papers are used to establish prestige —
How billboards help mail selling produce greatest results — Using publicity to coöperate in
limited territory.

XIV

USING THE MAILS TO KEEP CUSTOMERS SOLD.... 285
Statistics show why customers get away from
business houses — The value of a customer —
How claim adjustments are handled so as to

produce new business — New customers killed by the credit department, can be restored to life — Avoiding customer indifference.

XV

PLACE OF MAIL SELLING IN MERCHANDISING..... 307
Who can use mail selling methods — Raising funds for churches, schools and charitable institutions — Introducing new inventions — Statistics as a guide to sales plan — Sales inventories and what they show.

INTRODUCTION

I WAS greatly impressed some twenty years ago when connected with the retail store of Marshall Field & Company with the views of H. Gordon Selfridge, now of Selfridge's, London, and then General Manager of Marshall Field & Company, Chicago.

There were hundreds of charge customers on the books — in Chicago and all over the west and central west — who bought more or less at Field's. A check-up showed large annual purchases from some, only moderate buying from others, and a vast number whose trade was only spasmodic. The average purchases were lower than it was figured they should be.

It was pointed out by Mr. Selfridge that these lists of known people could be reached by mail regularly, systematically, and kept in close touch with the store, and the merchandise offered in a very personal way.

Such a proceeding is regarded now as a matter of course in any business, wholesale, or retail, large or small. At that time, however, the idea was rather startling. We had been accustomed to advertising in the newspapers and waiting on the people who happened to come into the store, and we hoped that they would come back when they wanted something else. To talk to them through the mails regularly was rather a radical innovation.

The development of this direct by mail solicitation fell into my hands and I was able to watch all angles of this sensational experiment. It worked. The results were so satisfactory that the company gradually increased direct advertising activities until today, approximately 33 per cent of the annual advertising appropriation is devoted to direct mail work.

I mention this experience here as parallel to the experiences of other firms in the retail and manufacturing field who have seen the tremendous influence of mail advertising grow, at first unaided and in fact, ridiculed, to a point when its sales value was recognized and then cultivated as one of the most important factors in selling.

The tremendous possibilities for increasing

business, and in this way reducing selling costs was thus first practically and thoroughly demonstrated to me at Field's. It opened up an opportunity to perform a real service to all engaged in merchandising by starting an organization equipped to render direct advertising assistance.

About that time I made the acquaintance of Mr. Merritt H. Dement, who was also fully impressed with the need for this service and its value to the advertising world. So about seventeen years ago the partnership of Buckley, Dement & Company was formed, rather short on capital, but long on ideas and enthusiasm. We knew we could render a helpful direct mail merchandising service to all engaged in marketing products.

Like every service of this kind, where the mind of the prospective patron has to be educated to his needs, the growth of the idea was at first slow. Yet, by using the methods that we advocated, we steadily advertised our own business. The net result has been a growth which has forced us four times to seek larger quarters, and which sees us at this time installed in our own six story steel and concrete building with facilities for taking care of a volume of business undreamed of at the time of our first organization.

The increasing demand for speeches on this subject of direct advertising, and the increased number of our own inquiries, have shown that business men are interested in merchandising by mail. Almost daily we hear from interested students of advertising. Their questions, and those which have always followed my addresses before groups of business men, suggested to me the possibility of anticipating the majority of these inquiries if I would publish a book, which would outline in a simple and practical way fundamentals behind the problems that have been presented to us, and how they have been solved.

The only reason I have never written a book of this character before is that I have never seemed to have the time to do it. But B. C. Forbes knows how to get what he wants out of people. When he decided that he wanted this done by having me write a series of articles for his publication, to be published subsequently in book form, I did like most people who are confronted with a task which has to be done — I found time and ways to accomplish what previously had seemed impossible.

The answers to these problems show how business men have been saved from making foolish expenditures of money for advertising. How sales plans that were completely out of balance have been evened up, how firms which were headed toward bankruptcy have been induced 'to change their plans and brought back on the road to success. How many old established firms which had been creeping along in a comfortable rut have been revitalized and given a spirit of aggressiveness which has led them on to great big things. How young firms starting out in business have been helped, how discouraged sales forces have been keyed up with new enthusiasm, and hundreds of other instances which show the vital connection between merchandising by mail and merchandising in the old established, personal contact way.

The thought in presenting these ideas to business executives, to advertising students, and to all who are interested in the advertising field, is that I may be of service in helping to eliminate mistakes which would be costly. I believe that my views may help to guide people who are earnestly studying to promote economical methods of marketing.

It is very natural that our business, in solving the merchandising problems of American manufacturers, wholesalers, and distributors, should have many calls for expert and specialized skill. To solve every problem unaided is more than the work of one man. In carrying on our work, we have attracted to and associated with us men who have special ability and organized knowledge along phases of the business, with which I am familiar in a general way.

These men of our staff have helped me in the compilation of this book, and I want to acknowledge in this chapter the valuable assistance received from:

Mr. Merritt H. Dement, my associate of seventeen years, thoroughly seasoned, and practical, one of the best known authorities on Mailing List statistics.

Mr. Flint McNaughton, author of many books on business, whose experience embraces direct advertising work in almost every line of merchandising.

Mr. David Meldrum, whose keen analytical

and editorial work has been applied with great success to the problems of our clients.

Mr. Robert Herz, a young man of extraordinary ability in fashioning uniformly successful selling plans.

Believing as thoroughly as I do, that marketing and merchandising by mail is a coming profession and one that requires the utmost skill of everybody connected with merchandising methods, I commend the consideration of the future chapters to you in the hope that some of the points somewhere will be helpful in realizing better results in the things you are attempting to do.

HOMER J. BUCKLEY

THE SCIENCE
OF MARKETING BY MAIL

CHAPTER I

THE EVOLUTION OF MARKETING METHODS

ONE of the greatest questions concerning the American people today, — the question that is demanding the attention of merchandising experts in every field more and more, — is the cost of distribution.

A graphic illustration of the way the public interest is focused on this problem was given in the New York Times, a conservative, independent newspaper, where an editorial appeared which endeavored to prove how largely merchandising methods are responsible for the high living costs.

The following story is quoted from this editorial:

" An Indiana woman was peeling potatoes. She cut into one that was hollow, and inside was a note from a farmer who had raised the potatoes.

The note read:

' I got 30¢ a bushel for these potatoes — how much did you pay for them? '

She wrote back:

' I paid $1.80 per bushel.'

The farmer sent her just one more letter. It read:

' I got 30¢ for those potatoes. It could not have cost more than 25¢ to carry them to you. Who got the other $1.25? I am going to try to find out! ' "

That story represents a very general attitude on the part of the public, the newspapers, the legislators, and even of the Government, who look with suspicion on all engaged in merchandising today.

The farmer referred to in the editorial had neither the information nor the experience to enable him to know just what it does cost the retailer and the produce man to handle his potatoes and deliver them to the consumer. What he did know was that he grew these potatoes, that they were no better when the consumer got them than when he parted with them, and that he got only 30¢ out of the $1.80

which the person for whom they were grown had to pay. He felt that he was entitled to a larger share of the retail price. The woman who had bought them felt she had paid too much for distribution, and very little for potatoes. She could not eat distribution.

If this distrust of the methods of handling goods were an isolated or exceptional condition on the part of the public, it would not be worth serious consideration, but the fact is that it is typical of the esteem in which the so-called middleman is held. Why should there be such distrust of a hard working and important class of people?

Time for Distributors to Wake Up

But, if the manufacturer and producer are concerned about the high cost of getting their wares to market, and if the consumer is incensed about the large proportion of the cost paid for distribution, what does this mean to those engaged in marketing?

It means that every person engaged in the distribution of merchandise is under close scrutiny, and their methods are subject to criticism. It means that economical methods are vital to their continued existence, for the public will not long tolerate extravagant, outgrown and costly marketing.

Those who insist that the only way to make a sale is to send the personal salesman, would, if their ideas were adopted, throw this country back over a hundred years in its merchandising. If every sale had to be made as a result of personal contact, the cost of selling would be tremendously increased, and such a vast force would be employed by every organization, that the transaction of modern business would be practically an impossibility.

From the report of the Joint Committee of the 67th Congress on Marketing and Distribution, I quote the following:

"We have now reached the point where it costs more to distribute and serve than it costs to produce. Commodity values are lost in a maze of service costs, and the time has come for a consideration of the fundamental problems of distribution."

That is one of the items of news that show the trend of the times. We must look for the reasons why things we buy cost so much, while things we manufacture or produce bring apparently such low figures.

This condition is not economically sound, and it is to the best interests of our future that we investigate, not only as a nation, but as associations, business houses, and individuals, and find out the reason back of the present unbalanced and inharmonious conditions and strive to bring about a more logical relationship between the cost of production, or producer's price, and the selling price of merchandise.

Unless those engaged in the distribution of merchandise earnestly seek to solve this problem, and remove from their activities the stigma of unfair or exorbitant costs, it is not unreasonable to suppose that measures will be taken by producers and consumers, or even by the Government, in an effort to reduce the exorbitant selling prices that prevail today as a growing menace to our prosperity.

It is imperative, therefore, that we look upon marketing by mail as a science which is just as important as the science of productive efficiency and as the science of accurate accounting, and consider it in the light of its relationship to the public need, and the service that it renders.

Merchandising by mail, when added to other

selling methods, not only increases the volume of sales, and consequently reduces the cost of selling, but in pushing weak lines, establishing new merchandise in the field, driving for business during dull seasons, building goodwill and developing a trade desire, it enables sales to be made on a profitable basis at all times.

Practical Proof of the Economy of Mail Merchandising

The history of marketing is filled with interesting examples of the development of quantity production made possible through mail methods, thus reducing selling price and creating profit.

The makers of a well known camera made one camera twenty-eight years ago which took a $2\frac{1}{2}$ inch picture and sold for $25.00. To-day they make a far better camera which sells for $10.00. A camera which took a 4 x 5 inch picture sold for $60.00 — a better camera today sells for $20.00. The reason is the cut in production costs made possible by the wide distribution secured through merchandising by mail.

Take as another instance a prominent hat manufacturer who by means of mail merchandising reduced his selling cost 7¢ per hat. The economic result of applying mail methods is that the buyer gets a hat of better quality without any increase in price, in spite of advanced cost of raw material and workmanship.

During the first year of operation the manufacturers of a well known watch sold 12,000 at $1.50 each. They did not advertise. The second year they did a little advertising, and they sold 87,000 watches.

The third year they used mail selling methods, and sold 485,000 watches. This means of merchandising gave them quantity production and they produced better watches and were able to sell them at a lower price.

This illustrates how mail methods increased the volume and lowered the cost of making sales. The same principles made use of in the above illustrations apply to any selling problem.

From 1914 to 1917, the cost of manufacturing an ironing machine increased 300%. Increased markets, obtained largely through the mails, enabled the product to be sold at a normal profit at a reduction in selling price, which brought it down to only 17% above 1914 levels.

A manufacturer of novelties had sold through salesmen exclusively for years. They applied direct mail advertising more and more because they found they could sell at less cost by mail. The change in their mode of selling, a gradual development, in this case, is typical in principle, if not in degree, of all manufacturers and wholesalers who find and apply scientific methods of selling by mail.

It has been the mail selling principle that has enabled Butler Brothers, a great Chicago jobber, to build up a mammoth business of $110,000,000 a year by mail, — that has enabled the Baltimore Mail Order House to sell $10,000,000 a year through two annual catalogs — without the assistance of a single salesman.

It is through this medium that life insurance companies have been able to reduce the cost of selling insurance from $23.10 per thousand exclusively by agents, to $11.63 per thousand when these agents are given advertising support. Records show that the Postal Life

Insurance Company sold life insurance last year at a cost of $2.95 per thousand.

The pioneer mail order house of Montgomery Ward and Company, Chicago, in selling to the consumer, has grown to mammoth proportions, and Sears Roebuck & Company, selling to the consumer by mail, has sold $246,000,000 of merchandise a year through their mail order catalog.

The amount of each actual first order received by mail order houses averages less than $15.00, and the traveling salesman's cost of making a call on a prospect is in most cases over $10.00. This shows the impossibility of making all sales by personal contact. These figures speak for themselves as to the economy of the mails to do marketing, and demonstrate that there is a field of business which personal selling cannot economically reach.

Only in recent years have financial houses countenanced advertising of any form as a means of promoting business, but as the result of effective mail methods that have become apparent, banks, bond and stock houses have applied marketing by mail to their various departments, and today, thousands of dollars are placed on saving deposits by mail; bond and stock issues are floated; trust departments built up and other functions of financial institutions promoted by mail methods of marketing.

Development of Trading Methods

Merchandising is a natural result of the evolution of business. It is a development that must constantly be adapted to the increasing complexity of the world's conditions. In the days of early trading where the farmer took his own produce and delivered it himself, his marketing problems were simple, but as men began to specialize and to produce things in quantity (which is in strict accordance with economic procedure) the matter of finding the buyer had to be entrusted to somebody else. This agent, buying in quantities, and assembling into huge stores, redistributed again to other people who would buy in small quantities, and sell to the actual consumer.

While it is customary to point to the middleman and to show his shortcomings, and the expensive methods of merchandising employed, the contrast must, indeed, be favorable when we compare him with the traders of the early days, whom we still find typified in many of the Oriental countries.

With the old merchants of Tyre, the Phoenician, the Arab, pioneers in the trading field, we find excessive costs of merchandising.

Compare their long journeys in small ships to distant lands to bring a scant cargo of merchandise, their long waits in the booths for a customer, and the long continued " haggle " of buyer and seller, both striving their best for a " bargain," with the methods of today.

But the merchant of today, who receives the benefit of economical transportation, whose store is the buying place for hundreds for every sale made by the Oriental merchant, and who can reach the ear of his prospects without necessitating their stirring from their fireside through mail merchandising methods has a sound and far more effective method of selling goods than had his ancient predecessor.

The Benefits of a Common Language

One of the most outstanding features of the record of American marketing is the unparalleled extent of its use of the printed and written word. To cover the same area on the continent of Europe, advertisements would have to be printed in forty or fifty languages whereas in these United States, the one language is universal, and permits of the widespread dissemination of information which enables millions of people to buy goods without actually seeing samples.

This is where the science of marketing by mail begins. It is the way in which the merchandiser can counteract the high cost of transportation of his traveling salesman by sending a printed message at a cost of a few cents, which enables the house to produce a far larger volume of business at a lower cost of selling. In many instances, the mail methods perform the entire function of selling goods direct by mail.

Let us not mislead ourselves, as so often we have a habit of doing, that American prosperity is due to the fact that Americans are the smartest people in the world. There are some wonderfully smart people from across the water. But let us realize the factors that go to make American prosperity, and then we shall see what we should do to retain our leadership, how we can improve our efficiency in handling merchandising problems so that we may continue to be leaders in the merchandising field.

If it were possible for the people in Europe to decide on a universal language, and to make use of merchandising by mail on the economic basis that we in this country have adopted, they would find that this fact alone would make a remarkable difference — in reducing their cost of doing business, and increasing their standards of living.

Buying Follows Desire

Those who imagine that merchandising consists only in producing a product at lowest cost have failed signally to recognize that human element in all trade — that a desire must first be created on the part of the consumer before a sale can be effected.

And how have these desires been created? Largely through the mails. We all know the value of general advertising — of the publicity in magazines and newspapers. That type of publicity and its vast educational power is obvious, but far less is known of those things that are not seen by the general public — the educative factors and direct selling methods of merchandising through the mails, producing immediate and direct results in sales and sales influence.

The purpose of this book is to show that the evolution of American business is just as much dependent on this current of advertising through the mails, which few see or know about, aside from the people addressed, as it is upon the announcements on billboards, newspapers, and magazines, those advertising factors with which everybody is familiar.

Nearly every one of the big things done in the field of marketing and merchandising by mail has been a pioneer event — something new and unprecedented. That is the reason why the evolution of marketing points more and more every day to the use of the mails as a powerfully effective means of distribution that no business house can afford to ignore.

Clients have come to us seeking counsel, we have analyzed the field, and found opportunities which had been waiting for years for development, and in a very few weeks, the campaign has been prepared and practically overnight it has spread itself throughout the length and breadth of the country.

Retail distribution has been revived with bulletins through the mails regarding saleable merchandise. Individuals have been educated to be better salespeople, local sales campaigns have developed trade. Consumer, retailer and jobber have been hooked up to the manufacturer in immediately effective mail campaigns. The results have been more goods sold, lower cost of selling, and goodwill built up. These plans invariably have opened up avenues of trade which have enabled the manufacturer to increase his volume of production, and in this way reduce selling costs.

We are just beginning to recognize the extent of these neglected opportunities, and this economic means of distribution in pointing a way for manufacturers to extend their business. If distributors will give due consideration to their merchandising problems, and realize the power of mail selling, we shall see, in the next generation, institutions so vast that by comparison the giants in business today will be mere pygmies.

In considering then the evolution of marketing methods, we must consider these factors.

THE FIVE DIVISIONS OF MARKETING

Research	Advertising	Merchandising	Selling	Distribution
Competitor's method analyzed.	Media Copy	Dealer education	Routing salesmen	Selecting territory
Dealer's volume of sales investigated.	Display	Counter displays	Mail announcements	Selecting credits
Questionnaires on selling methods.	Illustration	Window displays	Personal selling	Jobbers, brokers & wholesalers
	Frequency	Posters and signs	Direct-mail selling	Warehousing
		Direct-mail pieces	Teaching dealer how to sell	Transportation
		Samples		Containers
		Demonstrations		
		House to house canvass		

The mails are used in each of these five divisions of marketing. A glance at these subdivisions shows that the mails are highly important for most of these.

Development of Long Distance Markets

In the days of the pioneer, with the horse and wagon, or stage, it would not have been possible for the manufacturer located in the New England states to sell a pair of stockings in Pittsburgh without considerable expense for transportation.

The efficiency of railroad and motor truck transportation has made it possible for every manufacturer to increase his market beyond the limits which were possible to the old time methods of merchandising.

Today, manufacturers located half way across the continent send their products to market and compete successfully with the prices charged by competitors whose factories are right on the field.

The reason for this is obvious when we remember that the manufacturer at a distance is making use of the most economic forms of distribution that is possible for him to use, while the local factory restricting its output to local needs, does not get the benefit of low cost of modern methods of quantity production and distribution.

Larger Sales and Their Effect on Production Costs

The manufacturer, who sells his goods in a more extensive market, who has gone beyond the limitations of the firm whom his personal representatives can see, and who by working intensively, using every known sales methods, has boosted his volume of production, has done several things that are recognized as being economically sound.

He has used more up-to-date machinery, and in this way produced goods at lower cost.

He has reduced overhead by dividing the profit over a larger volume.

He has reduced markups by using more economical selling methods.

He has increased turnover by more energetically seeking business.

That brings us to the actual consideration of the purpose of this book.

The Fundamentals of Direct Selling Defined

If, as the investigation of a Committee on marketing and distribution in the United States Congress points out, an effort is to be made to reduce the high cost of distribution, we will never be justified in going back to the old-fashioned method of the small factory

AMERICAN BUSINESS

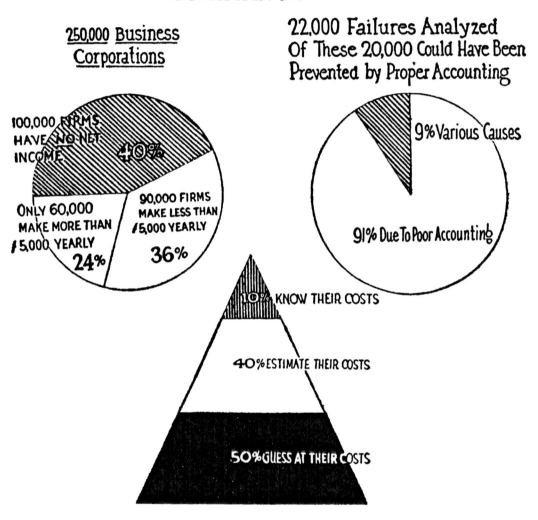

250,000 Business Corporations

100,000 FIRMS HAVE NO NET INCOME 40%

ONLY 60,000 MAKE MORE THAN $5,000 YEARLY 24%

90,000 FIRMS MAKE LESS THAN $5,000 YEARLY 36%

22,000 Failures Analyzed Of These 20,000 Could Have Been Prevented by Proper Accounting

9% Various Causes

91% Due To Poor Accounting

10% KNOW THEIR COSTS

40% ESTIMATE THEIR COSTS

50% GUESS AT THEIR COSTS

Federal Trade Commission Report

with a small clientele. That would be reducing the cost of distribution but increasing the cost of manufacture. The result in this case would be a tremendous economic loss. We cannot reduce wages or profits in production because that would lessen efficiency. We cannot secure raw materials at lower cost.

But there is a very great need to reduce the cost of distribution by giving scientific consideration to the factors that go to make sales, and by considering in its economic relations the most intelligent and least expensive means of educating people to values and standards — the printed word as exemplified by the progressive American advertisers.

So many vague and absurd ideas have existed in the past in regard to advertising direct by mail, that it is highly important to consider this matter in a plain and sensible way.

There is no more need to be clever or funny or freakish, bizarre or grotesque in selling by mail than there is in selling personally.

The most successful type of advertising is that which not only tells its own story well, but fits the prospective customer's desires.

The advertiser who can tell the story to the customer and connect it closely with his personal interest is the advertiser that produces results.

Likewise marketing by mail plans must be predicated on these same principles — your merchandising story interpreted in the language of the interest of the prospect.

When we get this same idea as our first consideration, it will be easy for us to eliminate much of the waste in advertising and selling which is now going on, and which is so evidently wasted from the outset because it tells a poor story in a freakish and grotesque way to people who are not at all interested.

Let us consider then in the following chapter some of the basic things in planning merchandising by mail.

Chapter II

MAIL SELLING PLANS BASED ON STATISTICS

IT has been said that when a plumber makes a mistake, he charges for it twice. When an attorney makes a mistake, it is just what he wanted as he gets a chance to try the case all over again. When a preacher makes a mistake, no one knows the difference. When a judge makes a mistake, it becomes a law. When a doctor makes a mistake, it is buried.

But when a business firm makes a mistake in their marketing and selling plans, it not only proves costly, but it may be the cause of wrecking the business, because the error in policy usually relates to an expenditure of capital which has gone over the dam never to return.

Therefore, the budgeting of expenses, according to a definite established plan and an analysis made as to the relations of expenses to sales by departments, is highly important in a business where the sales volume is attained either all or in part by selling by mail.

A budget establishes control, and control is nothing more than a business brain in action. Success depends upon the intelligence of the application and the ability to dominate and direct others in the performance of their tasks. The basis of all business judgment should be facts and figures.

The Importance of Facts and Figures in Every Business

An outstanding experience occurred a few years ago and covers this situation more effectively than any generalizing statement.

It came about as a result of an address I made on the subject: " Fundamentals of Marketing by Mail " before a jobbers' association convention at the Auditorium Hotel in Chicago. At the conclusion of my talk, one of the members followed me out of the convention hall and called to me for an interview. He introduced himself as the president of a well-established jobbing concern located in a small town in one of the Northern states and said:

" Young man, we are thinking about establishing a mail order department in our business and what you have said here today interests me very much. Would you be agreeable to coming up to our town and accepting an assignment to inaugurate the department for us? At the present time we are getting the bulk of our sales through salesmen making the larger towns, and the occasional sending out of printed circulars and catalogs in a haphazard, miscellaneous fashion — but we would like to work out a systematic marketing plan, especially to get after the small town business which our salesmen are passing entirely."

Arrangements were completed and I agreed to go up and spend several days with them to get the department organized and to give them two days a month for a period of a year. After my arrival at their offices, I requested that a meeting be called of the department heads and officers so that I might outline the background of a well-organized mail sales department and get the necessary facts and figures.

When I asked for a copy of their sales records, the sales manager brought it forward with a feeling of pride, for he had made a big increase in the year just closed. Hurriedly examining the records, I asked: " How many departments do you have? Let me see your department sales records." " We do not maintain sales by departments. Our system is daily sales, weekly sales, monthly sales, quarterly, semi-annually, and annually and as our salesmen sell all departments they are grouped together," was the astonishing reply.

When a business firm operating two or more departments tells me separate records of sales and expenses by departments are not maintained, I invariably ask to see their balance sheet for there is usually something fundamentally wrong with their methods.

Therefore, in the instance cited above, I asked for the balance sheet and a puzzled look came over the faces of those present, wondering what all this had to do with the inauguration of a mail order department, but, without hesitation, they brought out the statement requested.

It showed a substantial cash balance and a profit well up in the five figures for the year, and, apparently, all was satisfactory. Running my pencil down the item of fixed charges, I said, " I don't see any charge here for rent," and a quick response came back, " Why, no, we own this building." " Fine," I said, " how much is it worth? " " $60,000," was the reply. " Six per cent on $60,000 is $3600 per year. That is your rent." A dozen other similar deficiencies were found, no reserves of any kind set up for depreciation, inventories taken on an entirely wrong basis.

" Who does your accounting? " was my next question. " Our bookkeeper makes our statements and trial balance, and we have another bookkeeper, from a neighboring factory, come in every month and verify our trial balance."

" My recommendation, gentlemen, is that you do not start your mail order department until a complete check-up and audit has been made, and a budget control of expenses and sales by departments established, so that you will know definitely which departments are paying a profit and what merchandise we can push vigorously and be sure of a profit."

The net result was that at the end of two

days of tedious work with the assistance of a certified cost accountant, we had the facts and figures about their business. These figures developed surprises. Six of their departments were on a very satisfactory paying basis, while the three other departments were showing losses, and the one pet department of all of the sales force, from the sales manager down, had shown a $11,000 loss for the year, and this particular department had always been given more than half of the space in their catalog.

Radical changes were immediately made effective, and within a few months we were ready to proceed with the mail sales department, and today more than fifty per cent of the entire sales of this company is handled by mail. Marketing their products by mail is now on a scientific basis.

Costs Are the Keynote to Success

When Edward N. Hurley was Chairman of the Federal Trade Commission, he conducted an extensive investigation into the question of costs of doing business by manufacturing and business firms in the United

States. In an exhaustive report he summarized the whole situation with the startling statement that " The average American business man would do a whole lot better shaking dice." He made the assertions that most men in business were operating blindly, that more than fifty per cent of manufacturers, jobbers and merchants did not know their costs; that their selling prices were determined very largely on guesswork, and what their competitors were doing, without regard to the facts in their own business; and that many were operating at a loss at least in some departments of their business, and did not know it.

Costs are the " shibboleth " of the present day merchant. Few know how to get around them. Many have a record of labor costs, machinery costs, and are possibly able to determine with a fair degree of accuracy just what their factory cost is, and in some cases, they even add transportation costs. When they have obtained these costs, they in some way figure: " Well, the overhead, salaries, bad debts and selling costs will have to come out of profits." But serious consideration is seldom given to learn-

Figuring Profits

If a merchant, in marking goods for a certain per cent profit, has only the cost price to go by, he can find the selling price by subtracting the per cent of profit he wishes to obtain from 100. This shows the relation of the cost to the selling price.

For instance, an article costs $3.75 and the merchant wants to make a profit of 25 per cent. To find the price at which the article must be sold to realize this profit he first deducts 25 from 100. This gives a remainder of 75, the percentage of the cost.

If $3.75 is 75 per cent, 1 per cent would be 5 cents and 100 per cent $5.00, which, of course, is the price the goods should be marked.

A convenient table for the merchant in marking his stock is the following:

To make $16\frac{2}{3}$ per cent profit,
   add 20 per cent to the cost.

To make 20 per cent profit,
   add 25 per cent to the cost.

To make 25 per cent profit,
   add $33\frac{1}{3}$ per cent to the cost.

To make $33\frac{1}{3}$ per cent profit,
   add 50 per cent to the cost.

To make 50 per cent profit,
   add 100 per cent to the cost.

ing accurately what each one of those costs will be and how much profit should be allowed to provide a safe margin. The first basis for merchandising — and this applies to marketing by mail as well as to any other method of merchandising — is an accurate knowledge of costs of doing business. These can only be safely computed when all elements of costs are provided for, and a margin of profit established over and above the cost.

The costs in business cover all elements that enter into the thing sold — not only raw materials, labor, rent, power, equipment, but depreciation, interest and investment should be considered. Further, all costs should be departmentized, under different methods of merchandising. Staples, like sugar and flour, can be sold at a low margin between the actual cost of production and the retail price because there is no necessity to educate people as to their need for these staple articles. There is very little danger of spoilage, and there is very little likelihood that these articles will remain on the dealers' shelves unsold for any great length of time.

To speak in marketing terms, the markup

is small because the turnover is rapid and sure.

To most people engaged in the sale of staple commodities the facts regarding volume of sales are easy to obtain so that the actual selling and transportation costs, relationship to storage, rental, and all other expenses to the article sold are easily determined.

The situation is different, however, where the article to be handled is new. Then the public must have a period of time in which to judge it, an educational campaign must be run, dealers must be sold, and the whole process of establishing a market gone through. The selling costs in this case are abnormally high and they must be predetermined, or reasonably allowed for, before a sound merchandising plan can be approved.

How Selling Costs Are Determined

" How can you know ahead of time how much it is going to cost to sell each article you place on the market? " is a question frequently asked.

With an absolutely new article — entering
the field for the first time this must, of course,
be a matter of careful planning and calcula-
tion by making tests, etc., because no person
can foretell the public response to a merchandising appeal on an untried article.

The importance of accurately determining
selling costs has been brought home to us time
and time again when consulted on the question of marketing by mail, not only new
products, but also established businesses
operating over a period of time. A hundred
or more actual experiences could be cited
where our firm has had an opportunity to
analyze the facts which prove conclusively
the need of basing selling plans on statistics.

An instance that will make clear the situation is the case of an Indiana manufacturer.
A few years ago the manager of this particular concern came to Chicago with an
appropriation of $15,000 to spend in adver-
tising. His stockholders had reluctantly and
with many misgivings, voted this sum for an
advertising campaign to increase their sales.
He headed for one of the best known and
most successful advertising agencies. Fortunately, he had his interview with one of the

Need Business Fail?

Inexperience 4.7%

Specific Conditions 20.9%

Lack of Capital 30.8%

Incompetence 34.2%

The following table showing the failures and liabilities by percentages in 1922, tells a most interesting story:

FAILURES AND LIABILITIES BY PERCENTAGES IN THE UNITED STATES IN 1922

Failures Due to:	Number	Liabilities
Incompetence..........	34.2%	21.6%
Inexperience...........	4.7	1.9
Lack of capital.........	30.8	24.4
Unwise credits.........	1.3	1.5
Failures of others.......	1.2	2.5
Extravagance...........	.7	.6
Neglect...............	1.1	1.0
Competition...........	1.1	1.2
Specific conditions......	20.9	37.0
Speculation...........	.3	1.8
Fraud.................	3.7	6.5
TOTAL.............	100%	100%

85% of all failures could have been avoided by merchandising knowledge covering the three major factors of competency, capital and specific conditions.

This shows the importance of merchandising analysis. In merchandising by mail especially is this knowledge of vital importance.

keenest merchandising men in that agency.
After a half an hour's talk, the agency man
said to him: " Your proposition is not one of
general advertising. Your market is a limited and a restricted one, and can be covered
more economically and effectively in a mail
campaign. See Mr. Buckley, of Buckley,
Dement & Company. That firm specializes
in marketing by mail. Have a talk with
them."

In due time the man arrived and told us
about his business, which was manufacturing
mops and appliances for car cleaning and
industrial uses. He was anxious to inaugurate an advertising and selling campaign to
secure increased business. They had two
men traveling, representing them as a side
line, calling on railroad car shops, on a
brokerage commission basis, and they had
several good contracts which the principals
had lined up through personal connections
as the main nucleus of their business.

After hearing this outline, the very first
question put to him was: " How much does
it cost you to make your product per unit or
per dozen? " He looked at me rather surprised, and asked: " Will you tell me, just

what this has to do with advertising?
I'm here to develop a marketing and advertising campaign, not to discuss the production costs." But when we showed him that the relation of his costs to his selling price would determine how long he could stay in business, and whether or not he would show a profit or a loss, campaign or no campaign, he changed his attitude entirely. " Well," he said reluctantly, " we have a cost record which we have worked out by taking our payroll expenses and adding to it our material bills, and that gives us our factory cost. Our bookkeeper makes up the sheet for us every month."

Asked how he arrived at selling prices, he replied: " Well, when we started two years ago we canvassed the competitive field, and got hold of all other price lists, and we struck an average rate per dozen to put our selling price on a basis of equality with our competitors, although we have many improvements in our product which give us a selling advantage."

It's a tragedy of modern business to think that a manufacturer in this day and age would conduct a business in that way. But it goes to prove that Mr. Hurley was right. Our experience has proved that hundreds of business houses establish selling prices on what their competitors are doing and not on the sound business basis of costs.

If this same manufacturer had come into our office ten or fifteen years ago with $15,000 to spend in advertising we would have undertaken the work and he would have started back to his Indiana home, happy in the thought that his business was going to grow in leaps and bounds — only to be disappointed and face a huge loss within a year or two.

Today we know from experience, however, that the only successful way to build a business — no matter how good a marketing plan may be devised or how cleverly or effectively the advertising written and prepared — is to have the foundation of the business correct. The product itself must not only be right, but accurate and comprehensive cost records must be maintained and selling prices determined not only on the market or competitive prices, but on a schedule of, costs, pro-rated over a production basis of a specified volume. A campaign of marketing must be planned to make the scheduled quota so as to maintain the determined costs.

We did not recommend a marketing campaign of mail advertising to this manufacturer. In fact, we very positively advised him not to advertise until he got his foundation on a more solid basis.

He was keenly disappointed — for he had been living, breathing, dreaming, and thinking of this advertising campaign for a long time, and now that he was ready to go ahead, we were stopping him. Here's what we said to him: " Instead of spending that $15,000 in advertising now, set aside $500.00 immediately for a complete analysis of your costs, and let's get the facts about your business before we start any advertising." Reluctantly he agreed and we placed a cost expert in his factory, and within a week we had the full check up. It not only proved what we had suspected, but it brought to light conditions that enabled us then and there to make recommendations as to what he should do at once.

Costs were twenty-three per cent higher than he had thought — they were operating at a loss and did not know it. If we had gone ahead on a marketing campaign and increased their sales, the more business they developed the deeper they would have become involved. They would have eventually faced bankruptcy, notwithstanding that their trial balance showed a profit because it was only a paper profit.

The reports showed they occupied 20,000 square feet of floor space in a high-priced manufacturing building in one of the large Indiana cities. They were paying a high rate of rental per square foot and paying excessive drayage charges, both on raw materials from the freight depot to factory and the finished products to the freight houses. Their wage scale was high — much higher than all competitors except one. They had no reserves of any kind set up for depreciation, interest, taxes, bad debts, etc. They were losing ground although they made a good product and their orders repeated. Their product was their redeeming feature.

Our first recommendation was to get them to change the location of their business, and it was a battle to get them to see it. We sent a letter to Chambers of Commerce in fifty or more small towns within a radius of one hun-

dred miles, reading: " We have a client —
a small manufacturer employing fifty people,
who is desirous of locating in a town about
the size of yours.

What has your town to offer in the way
of a factory building that has side track
facilities, 25,000 to 30,000 square feet or more?

This business is a good one, and will give
employment to an increasing number of
people as it grows. Outside of eight or ten
people they will bring along with them, the
remaining help will be hired in the town in
which they locate. Please advise at once."

Thirty-five towns expressed a keen desire
to secure the factory and an offer was finally
accepted in a town twenty-eight miles distant
that gave them a factory building with three
years free rent and a nominal rate thereafter.
It was accepted and four months afterward,
the factory was in its new location.

Costs were reduced forty-six per cent
through lower rents, reduced wage scale, no
cartage and drayage costs, decreased insurance
rates, lower taxes and better conditions all
around. They had put their business in order.
Then the marketing and advertising campaign
started.

Does this not prove the relationship and the importance of costs and selling prices to any marketing and advertising campaign that might be promulgated? They are inseparable.

This was not an unusual instance. It is typical of conditions existing in many businesses all over the United States.

There are some 300,000 business concerns in the United States reporting to the Federal Trade Commission. Less than twenty per cent of this number are earning six per cent or better on their capital stock; more than eighty per cent are earning less than six per cent. We don't need associations to regulate selling prices in restraint of trade in this country. What we need for every business in this country is an educational program for a simplified, accurate, workable cost system. Then selling prices will take care of themselves without regulation.

How Volume of Orders Is Predetermined

To the person without manufacturing and merchandising training, it appears a tremendous gamble for a manufacturer to invest a large sum of money, and equip a plant to produce an article before sales have actually been made but it is not so to those who recognize that merchandising follows certain natural laws.

For example, a grocery concern, selling by mail from catalogs, had developed an annual business of $600,000. An analysis showed they had 10,000 customers on their books — average of $60 per year from each customer. The average order was $15, and the customer purchased four times a year. It was a simple matter of calculation to determine in advance how many new customers they must add in order to attain a volume of $1,000,000 per year.

Statistics are available on so many of the factors that enter into sales that the market can be forecast with a surprising degree of accuracy.

The manufacturer of a gasoline engine, through investigation, will find that 250,000 gasoline engines of a certain type are bought in the United States every year. Statistics show that sixty-five per cent of these engines are bought through dealers, and he knows that of the manufacturers selling through dealers, he has a certain number of competitors. With these and similar facts as a basis, the demand possibilities can be determined in advance, and the campaign launched with a definite volume of business in prospect.

Volume of orders should be based on a sales inventory of the consumers of the proper caliber in each territory. This consuming public may be those who now recognize the need for the product and are prospects for immediate business, or who are latent prospects, who will purchase only after an educational campaign sells them the idea.

How the Appropriation for Selling by Mail Is Determined

The cost of marketing by mail must be determined individually for each business by tests. There are many elements that influence results. No set rule can be applied. Experience is a valuable protection to advertisers.

There are many kinds of advertising. Conditions may make one kind more effective than another in any particular case.

In establishing businesses, a common plan

is to set aside a percentage of gross sales for advertising and to divide this appropriation up between the kinds of advertising that will be most effective.

The basis of most well-regulated selling is the cost per sale. In mail-order houses, where the average cost of first sales is $10, the appropriation required would be based on the number of new accounts that were sought. If 1,000 accounts are desired, an appropriation of $10,000 is needed.

The plan that usually works out in mail selling most economically is known as the two step system; first getting the inquiry and second, following up and selling the prospect.

A well known typewriter company, after tests, figures the average cost of direct mail inquiries at $8.00 and magazine inquiries at $10.00 each, with an average net cost of selling $15.00 each. With these statistics they compute the appropriation required, based on the number of buyers that their capacity can accommodate.

The use of statistics in merchandising, as outlined in the previous parts of this chapter, apportioning a definite percentage of the selling price for the cost of manufacture, adds a known percentage for overhead, an accurate amount for selling cost, and a further sum for profit. Using a definite system for predetermining these charges and the volume of orders is a fundamental of a well balanced business.

In arriving at the appropriation for marketing by mail, there are several factors to be considered, and they should all enter into the final determination of what that appropriation should be. The records of the previous year's sales can be taken as an index of the future year's activities.

The capacity of the factory has to be considered. The financial resources have to be weighed, and marketing conditions for the coming year surveyed with accuracy. In arriving at the actual appropriation, consideration must be given to the number and cost of orders actually produced by salesmen doing personal selling.

What territory has been covered? Can new territory be added to this method of selling without adding to selling costs? How many orders have been actually produced by mail? What has been the cost? What are the factory and financial limitations? Can present territory be worked more intensively by adding mail methods? To what extent have the direct mail pieces stimulated the buyer and increased the sales of the personal representatives.

In most lines of business, it is possible to get an accurate line on what these results actually are, or to map out the probable results very accurately. Then the wise executive will plan his expenses so that from any source of expenditure there will be a revenue which shows a satisfactory margin of profit. When merchandising by mail is applied intelligently, the cost of selling is reduced and profits increased.

CHAPTER III

THE ECONOMIC VALUE OF TRUTH IN MARKETING BY MAIL

HAVING decided from our analysis of cost and our estimate of possible sales, just what amount of money we shall spend in the particular field of merchandising by mail, the next thing to determine is how we shall proceed to prepare the mail advertising pieces.

The first factor in merchandising is to overcome sales resistance because until an article is known people always have a reason why they do not wish to buy it.

Distrust and Suspicion, Major Sales Resistances

The greatest thing to overcome in introducing any article to the public is the distrust which people evidence toward articles offered

46

for sale. It is particularly true that new things and new methods and new values are regarded not only with distrust, but with suspicion.

Until suspicion and distrust are removed, and the public has confidence in the article you are offering for sale, merchandising will be an impossibility.

Many years ago the policy of business was to barter " sight unseen." The policy of selling was " let the buyer beware." This policy, which has developed from the ancient times, was reversed a few decades ago, by a daring retailer. The policy was established, that " The customer is always right." The plan was discredited by competitors of " You must be satisfied " as universal. It removes resistance to selling and is possible because there is value in the goods and truth in advertising is possible.

One mail order house has found that they are imposed on in only a fraction of one per cent of sales through their policy of " money back if you are not satisfied, or if you think the merchandise is not right." The experiences of other mail order houses are similar.

Most students when they first enter the

advertising field are imbued with the desire to do something novel. They think that advertising calls for clever and exaggerated statements, for novel and freakish ideas, for loud, bizarre, and contrasting colors.

These efforts of the amateur to force sales by the method of the clown or the braggart actually defeat the opportunity of the merchant to place his goods before the public in a favorable light.

The first fundamental in merchandising by mail for the producer, jobber, and wholesaler is the appreciation that it pays to tell the truth.

Time was when business men were afraid to admit that any articles they were selling were seconds, or were defective in any way, but, fortunately, the tendency in later years is to admit defects where there are defects and to tell the truth about them, at the same time offering real reasons why the merchandise offered is an exceptional value.

This policy of truth is the only sure method of building confidence and destroying distrust and suspicion which is the bar to selling.

The business man who tells the truth in such an earnest and impressive way that none of his hearers can mistake the sincerity of his message, impresses all those who come in contact with his merchandise and his methods with the fact that his store is reliable.

Confidence in the Customer a Demonstrated Success

The most conclusive demonstration of the value of a principle is its continued success. The principle of " truth in marketing " has been demonstrated by the most notable examples in all divisions of merchandising activity.

Montgomery Ward & Company, and Sears Roebuck & Company, demonstrate the success of the policy of a truthful representation of goods in the mail order to consumer field. They typify the successful merchant using this method of marketing.

Two of the best known retailers, Marshall Field & Company, of Chicago, and Wanamaker's of Philadelphia (who use large quantities of mail matter in merchandising), stand for the principle of honest representation of honest merchandise, and their success has been phenomenal.

So we see that all types of merchants attain success when they adhere to " truth in advertising."

With the factor of truth definitely established, as the basis in a plan for marketing by mail, we must consider that the principal reason for deciding on a policy of truthfulness is to establish confidence as opposed to distrust.

We know that confidence increases as the result of long establishment. When people in Philadelphia say of anything they have bought: " It comes from Wanamaker's," they have expressed the confidence that they have in that store which through many years has developed an enviable reputation for square and honest dealing.

But, where a policy of misrepresentation is pursued, the career of the house is sure to be a short one and the end to be in bankruptcy or failure. As the years go on, these two policies assert themselves — either a house must build up a reputation which wins the confidence of the public, or it must build up a reputation which means ultimate destruction.

In most of the old established lines of

merchandise, this word of misrepresentation is not necessary, but in so many of the newer businesses as in the younger industries — the tendency to misrepresent with the thought of making quicker sales is so flagrantly evident that it is necessary to impress these fundamentals on all who consider merchandising by mail.

Particularly is this tendency to misrepresent prevalent at the present time in the second-hand automobile industry, where the number of cars offered for sale " just as good as new " is becoming a factor in the industry.

Persistence in Mail Selling Necessary To Bring Results

Just as the public has no confidence in the " fly by night " concerns, and just as it looks with suspicion upon the new venture in the merchandising field, so does the first mailing piece sent out by a company to people who have never heard of it, fall upon unresponsive hearts and minds.

The number of manufacturers of new products who believe with childlike faith that the public is just waiting with open arms to welcome the product they are going to market is legion.

Ask any man who has patented an invention, and he can see, in his mind's eye, the customers come falling all over themselves to take advantage of the great boon he is to bring them.

It is a blow to many of these earnest men when they find that instead of being crowned with the laurel wreath as the savior of his country, the man who endeavors to market a new article is looked upon with hostile suspicion, and the public adopts a " show me " attitude.

Consequently, many people get discouraged after feeble attempts to merchandise in this way and discontinue efforts at the very time that the advantages of the initial efforts are available.

The country is full of people who will tell you that " I have tried direct mail methods of selling " because they have sent out one or two circulars on the article they are marketing. The man who would not think of renting a store for one month only, and then growing discouraged as a result of his first month's business, expects that a one-day try-out in the marketing by mail field is going to either make or break him.

It is not human to suppose that any method of merchandising can be found which will over-night banish all the distrust which people have toward a new product, and will place the new merchant on the same plane of confidence as the one who has been established for years.

The necessity for persisting in direct mail efforts, for keeping it up week after week, and month after month, until the confidence of the public has been unquestionably established, is just as necessary a fundamental of business as is the fact that a man must stay in business day by day before the public will have confidence in him.

Very few stores are rented for less than a year. Yet how many firms today are making advertising appropriations for a year?

The way to success in advertising is to decide on the fundamentals, to establish as your policy the telling of the truth in regard to your merchandise, and then to " fight it out " on that line if it takes all summer.

Goodwill Promoters Must Be Truthful

The chief asset of any business is its goodwill, and the promoters of goodwill are the points of contact between the firm and the person who buys from it.

Just as the untruthful clerk in the store, the traveling salesman of doubtful veracity, the department head of questionable conduct, and the other weak moral characters have been eliminated by wise business managers, so the untruthful advertisement in the newspapers, the unscrupulous announcement sent through the mails, and the letter which does not ring true are being eliminated from the advertising man's category.

Many of the merchants who have admitted that, " It's a good thing to keep your name before the public " — thus realizing the value of good will — pay so little attention to the character of the mailing matter sent out that they are being continually misrepresented and their business injured, by sending out the wrong type of letter, circular, or advertisment.

Remember that people have only one way to judge an organization, and that is by the points of contact they receive such as the personal call, the public announcement, window displays, and the merchandising by mail. All of these, because they are personal, leave the strongest impression in the mind of the recipient.

The statements in this chapter, while directed in their language toward building up the confidence of the public in the merchandise of the retailer have the same application when referred to the goodwill of the dealer for the manufacturer, or the goodwill of the retailer for the wholesaler. The confidence of the person who buys is the ultimate objective of all correspondence and advertising through the mail and truth is the essential in creating and holding this confidence.

Chapter IV

USING THE MAILS TO MAKE SALES

THE marketing of all manner of merchandise and service by mail has become so firmly established and so vitally a part of our commercial life that we seldom consider it as the most recent development, which it really is, of sales promotion.

The spectacular successes of some of the larger mail order houses selling direct to the consumer — notably Sears, Roebuck & Co., Babson Bros., and Montgomery Ward & Co. of Chicago, National Cloak & Suit Co. and Chas. Williams Stores of New York, have caused many people to believe that the " Mail Order to the Consumer Plan " is the most economical method of marketing and merchandising for every line of business and for every type of product.

The nation-wide publicity campaigns conducted by these big mail order houses, have developed the impression in the minds of many inexperienced merchandisers that mail order selling *always* has existed, whereas, as a matter of fact, all these institutions and indeed mail order selling itself, may be said to be a development of the last thirty years.

It is not surprising, therefore, that there are many phases and features of selling by mail with which the man on the outside is in no sense familiar.

There is a great deal of confusion existing in the minds of many people as to the term " mail order " and " promoting sales by mail." There is a distinction and a difference. " Selling by mail " is not a term synonymous with the mail order business. To sell by mail does not necessarily mean that you get the order by mail accompanied by that famous phrase " Enclosed please find check." Thousands of firms — manufacturers, jobbers, retailers and service organizations — are selling by mail while several thousand, more or less, are doing a mail order business.

An increasing number of business houses are using the mails to develop sales, though actually they rarely get a dollar's worth of business by mail order. A more correct and more comprehensive term for sales promotion of this kind would be " Direct Mail Advertising." These business houses, banks, brokers and merchants invest many thousands of dollars every year in letters, folders, catalogs, broadsides and many other forms of direct mail advertising for the definite purpose of educating the prospect and selling him as to the merits of the product or service. The pieces are planned to develop an inquiry, to bring the prospect into the place of business or to pave the way for the salesman's calling later. This phase of using the mails to make sales has had a very great development during the last twenty years, and it holds out inducements worthy of consideration by any firm having a commodity or service to market at a price.

Selling by mail can, and often does, mean getting the order by mail — doing a mail order business where the full burden of the sale is placed on the written word. This to me is the most interesting and fascinating of all methods of merchandising and in spite of the fact that it has been improved greatly in thirty years, nevertheless, it has tremendously undeveloped possibilities.

The Mail Order Business — Its Merits and Limitations

Thousands of people with the haziest idea of what mail selling is think there is some " white magic " in the name " mail order business." Since the advent of the automobile, especially, thousands have provided accessories more or less ingenious and useful, especially for the Ford car, and feel, in their lack of experience, that the problem of marketing the product is one of minor importance. Unless properly counseled, they undertake to sell these accessories, and very often meet with disappointment and failure.

With an occasional item, it has been possible to market successfully by mail, but most of these ideas are impossible for economic reasons that are evident to most people.

For instance, a man has a new type of gas-saving appliance which can be attached to the spark plug of a Ford car. He wants to sell it at twenty cents. The cost of manufacture is about eight cents. His average sale will be a set of four for eighty cents.

To reach the Ford owner by mail, with any type of presentation would require at least four cents per mailing so that reaching 10,000 prospects would cost $400.00. Even on a very exceptional proposition, the returns in actual orders could not be expected to exceed 10 per cent or 1,000 orders at eighty cents, a total of $800.00.

The cost of manufacturing on the 1,000 orders would be $320.00, and the cost of storage, wrapping, etc., would easily be $150.00 more, clearly a loss instead of a profit, even figuring on the most optimistic basis of returns.

When these facts are shown to prospective customers they wonder why it is possible for the large mail order houses to sell similar articles, and items costing even less money by direct mail methods. The answer to this is a demonstration of that well-known principle of merchandising — making group sales.

The mail order house performs a real service by combining a group of articles in one catalog. It presents merchandise inexpensively and permits sales to be made to remote parts of the country, to homes which are never effectively reached by the advertising of the regular retailers and homes where members of the family infrequently go to the city to see merchandise displayed.

The mail order house can effect sales in an economical way because it groups together its merchandise both for purposes of advertising and for purposes of shipping and transportation, and it makes shopping from the rural districts easily possible, and draws trade from the great masses outside of cities. It builds up a new line of business which would not be possible without the functioning of the mail order house.

But, as previously demonstrated, the functions of mail order merchandising cannot be applied to an article of merchandise irrespective of its cost. There are many commodities which can be sold through the mail, direct to the consumer, and they are being successfully sold in this way right along. But it must be remembered that the mail order house faces the economic principle of making profit out of every sale. Where the cost of doing business is greater than the profit, and there is no frequent repeat order to follow the initial sale, then profitable mail order merchandising becomes an impossibility

There is no department of modern commerce in which the reward is GREATER in proportion to time, effort and capital invested than in the mail order business.

Mail Order Methods that Have Won

The writer once had occasion to come in close contact with a wholesale grocer who had built up a large business selling through salesmen. As an analysis had shown a gradual falling off in profits over a number of years, and a constantly decreasing margin on their line, it was decided that the selling policy of the house should be entirely changed. Instead of selling to grocers it was decided to conduct a mail order grocery business direct to consumers.

In making this revolutionary change in selling plans, the house sacrificed a considerable asset of several thousand established and active dealers which it had spent years in winning as customers of the house.

An analysis of the conditions indicated that they would be able to sell groceries direct to housewives at exceptionally attractive prices, and that such a method of doing business would have advantages over the marketing plan that had been followed in the past.

After consideration, it was decided that the so-called two-step plan of mail selling to get in touch with the consumer and place their catalogs would be most advantageous for their use. A carefully prepared letter was sent to a list of one million women, located in the country and in the small towns, featuring the grocery catalog, and showing how much they could save by buying their groceries from them at wholesale. A return postcard worded as an invitation to send the catalog was enclosed, making it easy for the interested housewife to secure the catalog, listing the new line of groceries.

The mailing of 1,000,000 letters produced 135,000 inquiries for the catalog, and these catalogs placed with the interested housewives developed 40,000 customers within a year's time. The check-up on the business after a period of several months showed the average initial cost of orders to be $5.35 and it is well proven experience of all mail order selling that it is repeat business that makes the mail order business successful.

A mail order business that does not have

a repeat sale cannot be successfully conducted unless the selling price of the article is high enough to return satisfactory profit on each individual sale. To do this it is necessary that there be a long margin to cover the the relatively high cost of initial selling and render a satisfactory profit.

The reader should be impressed with this fact right here: The mail order business is for the WORKER not the SHIRKER. It is a business which demands the best thought and most careful preparation on the part of all who desire to enter it and who expect to achieve success.

The successful development of a mail order business for any line of merchandise requires just as intensive study and frequently just as large an investment as merchandising through the regular channels of business — the wholesaler and dealer. The success of mail order houses has not been immediate or phenomenal except in those rare instances where some unusual opportunity has presented itself to the mail order merchant.

Most successful mail order businesses have been built by steady and persistent effort on

MAIL ORDER HOUSES INVADE THE BIG CITIES

The convenience of merchandising by mail is demonstrated by the fact that the large mail order houses are no longer regarded as the source of only rural supplies. Quite a large number of city and suburban buyers patronize the mail order houses and use the mail methods of buying.

The ad illustrated above, clipped from one of the Chicago newspapers, shows how Sears, Roebuck & Company are extending their sales by selling right in their own city direct by mail.

sane lines of educating the prospective purchaser by mail to his need of the article
presented, and by steady, persistent merchandising efforts after the sale was made to
secure the recommendation of customers to
their friends.

The money that has been lost in the mail
order business was lost, in nine cases out of
ten, from no other cause than the lack of
common sense, in the proper planning,
preparation and analysis of the market.
You can't play the mail order " game " like
you do a gambling game and have any greater
chances to win. You can't take a blind
plunge into advertising and expect to achieve
success. All that is demanded of you in the
mail order business, is just the careful,
thoughtful, methodical application of common
sense. Don't invest a dollar in advertising
until your proposition has been studied and
analyzed from every angle and a selling plan
has been devised which you feel is " fool
proof." Don't start out on your advertising
program to develop inquiries until your follow-up is all prepared and printed and ready
for immediate use when the inquiries begin
to come in.

Use caution in the selection of your advertising media and in the preparation of your printed matter. Make tests as you go along to determine whether or not you are on the right track.

Don't spend all your money the first month — feel your way carefully and hold back a reserve fund, always, to tide you over the introductory period when orders and cash will necessarily come in more slowly than after your business has gained momentum.

Profit and losses pile up rapidly in the mail order business. In the effort to check loss and turn failure into success it is easy to pile up an aggregate loss of thousands almost before you know it, but when once the profits start coming your way, they roll into a fortune for you with equal speed.

Comparison of Retail and Mail Order Selling

Notwithstanding some of the outstanding successes that have been made in the field, mail order selling direct to the consumer is limited. Statistics show that eighty-five per cent of the business of the country is still done through the regular retail channels and less than fifteen per cent is sold by mail order methods. Thus the manufacturer, looking for the largest market for his goods in seeking to build up his business will turn his attention rather to the eighty-five per cent instead of the fifteen per cent of possible business.

There are 125 mail order houses in the United States doing ninety-five per cent of the mail order business. There are 1,250,000 retailers in the country. There are three or four million clerks and merchants backing the organized efficient mail order system of selling. About ninety-seven per cent of the retailers in America are not making any profits. They are falling down because they don't go after business and sell their localities in the same efficient way in which the mail order houses do.

They don't sell more goods and make more profits because they don't appreciate the need for systematic salesmanship, or they don't know how to go about it. They haven't been educated by manufacturers as yet to high enough standards, and the average dealer isn't a " self starter."

It is estimated that retail dealers in the

United States are doing an annual business of around $13,000,000,000. Mail order houses, on the other hand, are doing approximately $500,000,000 annual business. Only four per cent of the business of the country is done by the exclusive mail order houses. That makes the mail order business more than $10,000 for each state in the Union.

The states of Pennsylvania and Iowa are considered the best mail order states in the country, and the amount of mail order business done by the big mail order houses with the people of these two states is enormous.

The mail order business in the United States has grown rapidly. On the other hand, within the last few years there has been a gradual and very distinct stimulus in efficiency of advertising among retailers, which is effected by the helps and dealer aid plans of the highly trained and efficient sales organizations of manufacturers whose goods they sell. The progressive retailer has a tremendous sales advantage in sales helps, displays, national advertising, direct mail advertising and literature hook up plans. It has been demonstrated time and again by taking advantage of these possibilities that exist for the benefit of the retailer, any retailer can build up his local business to a gratifying degree.

How Dealers Are Sold Large Shipments of Merchandise Through the Mail

Probably, one of the largest wholesale businesses in the world has been built up by using the mails to merchandise the article it handles to the dealers of the country.

The name and reputation of Butler Brothers, Chicago, is known wherever there is a general store, and all of their merchandise has been sold to dealers through the mail. Their annual business is about $110,000,000.

I am not advocating this method as one all wholesalers should follow but I am pointing to it as an example of how a business can be built to gigantic proportions without the necessity of personal salesmen.

Other wholesale houses, and in fact, nearly all of them, sell a large part of their merchandise by means of mail order methods. Other firms which could advantageously use the mail for merchandising are neglecting this field and relying solely on their salesmen to produce business.

When a large wholesale book, stationery, and novelty house was confronted with the fact that in spite of an improvement in general business conditions, their own volume of trade was falling off, that the number of their dealers were decreasing instead of increasing, and that those dealers who were sending them orders were sending them smaller orders instead of larger ones, they called a conference of the sales executives.

Reports from the salesmen on the road indicated that rival houses had been getting orders because they had sent out bulletins and other advertising pieces, and because their catalogs showed better illustrations and descriptions.

The outcome was an immediate appreciation of the value of the type of advertising sent through the mail, and the firm entered whole-heartedly into the matter of re-establishing their prestige in this particular field.

The result of their investigation showed not only a lack of advertising support of their salesmen, but a field of uncultivated retailers — people on whom their salesmen had never called.

The effectiveness of the methods of merchandising by mail was shown when the compilation of the list of dealers revealed more than twice the number of actual retailers in the territory which was supposedly completely covered by the personal salesmen.

By establishing regular monthly mailings, and by humanizing the catalog, the firm was able to add to its list hundreds of new dealers and to stimulate the volume sent in by old dealers so that the total aggregate business received a tremendous impetus.

That is one instance out of many in various lines, which shows the absolute necessity of merchandisers using methods in their selling to which the public has proved responsive.

If the advertising for any merchandiser is handled right, the retailer will not wait for the call of the personal salesman, but will send in orders even amounting to thousands of dollars through the mail.

Not only does this apply to those houses which have a large variety of merchandise to sell, but it also applies to specialized lines. This plan of marketing is well stated in an article in the New York World:

" Until we made a determined effort to build our business, we never realized how much trade we were losing," said the sales manager of a large Philadelphia wholesale house. " We have always assumed that our big force of traveling men — 150 of them — covered the field thoroughly. Now we know that many an order was placed elsewhere between the salesmen's calls.

" We began by issuing a new catalog — one modeled on the lines of those issued by the big mail order houses — with every device included for making it easy to place orders. Appropriate pages of perforated postcards were bound in the book. Sheaves of order blanks were included.

" Then we assailed the problem of securing the coöperation of our salesmen. We explained that our plan was to secure more sales from each customer, and that this logically would increase the commission of each man.

" Between calls, your customers are inclined to place orders with competitors, we argued. Persuade them to use the catalog, and you will find many sales credited to you for which you have never worked.

" This made a strong impression.

" Our aggressive campaigns for mail orders have accomplished good results. Not only have they increased our gross sales over twenty-five per cent but they have added stability to our business — centralized control at the home office and weakened the salesman's personal control of the territory."

In the automotive equipment field, the firm which is probably the largest jobber of its kind, handles its dealers almost exclusively through the mail.

Whether the merchandiser is himself a manufacturer, a wholesaler, or conducting a chain of stores, the possibilities of merchandising through the mail are just as great. The principle involved is the same, as the confidence of the dealer in the person from whom they are purchasing is the essential thing in the making of large sales possible.

In introducing a new line to dealers, the most important thing for the establishment of confidence is for the dealer to see how his sales are to be made. Contrary to the belief so deeply embedded in some merchants' minds, it is not always the personality of the salesman which makes the sale, but it is the type of presentation which makes a dealer realize a real merchandising opportunity.

This presentation of the sales value of an

article, the story of the helps given to dealers, the reliability of the house, and the other factors which enter into the building up of confidence between the dealer and the wholesaler, or dealer and manufacturer, can be just as effectively told, in some cases more so, with a printed and illustrated story than it can by word of mouth from the personal salesman.

Time and again I have seen evidence of the fact that salesmen with personality and proven selling ability have been calling regularly on trade, but they have failed to produce the maximum volume of orders.

But when to the personality of the salesman and the excellence of the goods are added the force and effectiveness of well thought out direct advertising and well prepared illustrations, they have reached a much higher quota.

How Dealer Business Is Held and Stimulated by Mail Efforts

Any jobber or manufacturer who gets all, or nearly all of his business through salesmen is not making the most of his opportunities.

This not to the discredit of salesmen. They are necessary and they do good work, but the fact is plain that mail sales promotional methods, supplementing salesmen, develop a larger volume of business, build good-will, and lower the cost of selling.

No matter how good a salesman may be he will not be able to get all of the trade in his territory to which his house is entitled. His visits are too infrequent. Competition is too strong. It is asking too much of a retailer to ask him to hold his order until the salesman can come around again.

Unless the retailer is educated to order by mail from the campaigns sent out by manufacturer and wholesaler a great many good business opportunities will be neglected. Unless he takes advantage of the salable merchandise presented to him in these campaigns, he is going to miss a lot of business.

In talking with a salesman with one of the largest hardware concerns, he told me that when he goes into the store of a retailer he features certain specialties and sells all that is required. He recognizes there is a limit to the merchandise that a good retailer can buy at one time and only trys to sell him that quantity.

This salesman tells the dealer he will not be around again for several months, and leaves with him a catalog and price list and a number of postcard order blanks. He asks the retailer to send in mail orders to the house as often as he has enough " cuts " to warrant a shipment.

Within two weeks after the initial shipment arrives, the retailer usually needs more goods, and they are ordered from the catalog. Reminded periodically, by mail from the house, he sends in orders every few weeks. These orders would go to competitors if no use of direct advertising was made to support the salesmen in his territory.

The retailer's version of this is told in the following:

" By ordering from the catalog and the monthly bulletins sent out by a certain jobber, supplementing the calls of the salesmen, which average maybe four a year " said a hardware dealer, " I succeeded in turning my stock six or seven times a year in one department. I am helped to accomplish this by the sales suggestions and helps sent me by the house."

Modern merchandising is compelling the retailer to buy more and more of his needs

by mail. The mail order method of purchasing has developed among retailers almost
as much as among consumers, but in the case
of a retailer the plan is practically a necessity.

A well known cracker company in Kansas
City has a hundred salesmen making calls on
fifty per cent of their dealers once a week,
the balance once every two weeks.

The policy of this company is to send a
mailing to the dealers each month, giving
something of educational news value. The
regularity of the mailing sent every month,
or oftener, should be given some credit for
influencing business. It is their claim based
on actual experience, that the followup helped
to keep old customers " sold " as well as to
pave the way to new business.

It costs money to place and keep the name
of a dealer on the books of a manufacturer
or jobber, and it is wisdom to insure the
investment with advertising.

He has either accepted the representation
for the line because of the influence of a personal salesman, who has made a trip at a high
cost in railroad fare, hotel bills, and drawing
account, or he has responded to some ad-

vertising or mail appeal which has usually cost a few dollars for each dealer that responded.

And after the dealer has accepted your line, and has your goods in his store, and is presenting them to the public, your rivals are busy with their line, making representation of the profits he can make handling the agency for them.

That dealer has cost too much money to let him get away from you without making some effort to retain him as your representative.

He will retain and stand by the line he can make the most profit selling. Experience has shown that the most profit is to be made on the article that moves fastest. Suitable mail order plans will help to move merchandise faster for the dealer.

If the public demands your competitor's stove because it has never heard of the brand you manufacture, the dealer's preference will be for the other stove.

But you know that the article you manufacture is the better product, and if it is presented right it will sell in preference to that of your rival.

The logical thing to do then is to study

the selling methods which make the public demand the other stove, and apply those same methods in your case.

The moment a dealer accepts the representation for your goods, he becomes your partner. It is up to you to help him in every way that you can to dispose of the article you have asked him to sell.

Take an interest in his welfare. See that he is supplied with the proper window trims. Write to him once in a while with suggestions as to how he can increase his sales of the article with which you have supplied him. Instruct him so that he will become a more efficient merchant. Inspire him with some of your own confidence in the line. Keep him enthused over its good points so that when customers come in he will sell them enthusiastically and with confidence rather than merely show the goods and accept orders.

All of the good points of manufacture, all of the fine work of organization in establishing dealer representation, and all of the effects of general publicity will be lost absolutely if your rival beats you at the game by the aggressive sales presentation right on the firing line of the point of contact between dealer and customer.

I know of the case of one furnace company which had dealers established through 26 states, whose produce had points of merit of the very finest, and whose representation from the manufacturer to the dealer was excellent from the point of getting the dealer to accept the agency.

But until he had prepared and placed in the hands of his dealers a definite sales manual, showing how the goods should be displayed, how they should be advertised, how the sales talk should be made, and the other necessary features of making sales right to the customer, the sales plan had failed to produce the maximum results.

Aided by this type of helps through the mail, this stimulus and enthusiasm from the head office, dealers, instead of becoming mere representatives, whose stores act as a store-room for merchandise, became real salesmen who went out after the business hard and by interesting prospects and closing the sales of those who came in to inquire they backed up the manufacturer with a volume of sales, which meant real representation.

Showing the dealer how to make sales is coming to be recognized as one of the very important phases of any merchandising campaign, and there is no way in which it can be better accomplished. Through the mail, a constant stress of educational propaganda will reach the dealers and arouse in them an interest in your house and the goods you are producing.

Many salesmen recognize the need for helping the dealer sell, and the most successful salesmen are those who sell the dealer not new stocks of merchandise but plans for selling the merchandise which he already has on hand so as to make room for more.

Coöperating with this spirit of helpfulness, your mail merchandising plans should be plans which are predicated on stimulating the dealers' sales.

CHAPTER V

MANUFACTURERS WHO HAVE BE-COME MERCHANTS BY MAIL SELLING

A COMMON mistake of the novice in merchandising is to judge the success of the prominent men in this field of endeavor by the outward, visible and obvious evidences of their activities.

It is quite natural, therefore, that many people should seek to emulate the success of our large manufacturers whose names have been blazoned before the public in national magazines, on billboards, and in newspaper advertising, with the full and confident belief that by pursuing the same course in regard to their products they will achieve similar success.

The imitators fail at success because they only go part way and do not complete the sale. They spend a lot of money for the first part of selling — advertising — and most of this effort is wasted because the last part of the sale has been entirely neglected.

A very clear exposition of this fact was related by Mr. J. F. Older, mail sales manager of Armour & Company, at a convention of the Associated Advertising Clubs of the World in Atlantic City. Mr. Older told of some of the merchandising facts that have made his company one of the leading merchandising factors in this country. It was a revelation to many old and ex-advertising men to learn that although Armour & Company were spending about a quarter of a million dollars in newspaper advertising, they were spending twice that amount, or about $600,-000 for direct by mail work, show window material, dealer helps, and other similar means of merchandising their national advertising.

Armour & Company today have established their name and their product not merely by means of advertising, but because they have thought in the terms of the dealer and have helped the dealer to be a better merchant.

Unless the manufacturer of today can regard his product in this light and make himself, first of all, a merchandiser of his product right up to the time of the sale to the ultimate consumer, he must of necessity lag in the race when he is confronted with the energetic activities of those manufacturers who think the thing clear through.

To make a list of the manufacturers who use the mails to merchandise their product by dealer helps would be merely to list the names of the most successful concerns in the country, and yet it is strange that so many manufacturers have failed to see the necessity for merchandising their products and have never awakened to the potentiality of merchandising by mail and establishing their lines in the mind of the buying public.

Any manufacturer who inaugurates an advertising and sales promotion campaign today without a careful analysis of the market, is speculating with results.

I can best convey my thought by relating an experience which I believe will illustrate my point.

A manufacturer of washing machines had believed that the only practical method of selling washing machines was the old fashioned well-known method used practically universally for many years. That method was to sell the dealer and let him sell the consumer. This manufacturer found himself up against a hard proposition. Few dealers were merchandisers equal to forcing a demand for relatively high priced household specialties. The dealer wouldn't stock heavily even should the manufacturer sell him; if he did, he would be " stuck."

Let it be understood that there is no better, more convenient or desirable washing machine made today than the machine made by this particular manufacturer. The right kind of salesmanship would easily sell the machine to the dealer. This manufacturer came to us with a bundle of catalogs, literature and price lists. He laid the problem on the counsel table. He was skeptical but knew that there must be some way to move machines from the retailers' stock rooms.

A plan was arranged through our assistance which completely reversed the old method of selling. Where formerly the burden of distribution was put on the dealer, the new plan went further. It helped the dealer and his clerks. It was a simple and effective method for reaching the consumer through local advertising, and a plan for following up prospective buyers systematically.

The result was an increase of twenty-five

per cent in sales within two months. Eighty per cent out of every hundred women who came into the dealer's store for demonstrations walked out of the store unsold under the old system. Under the new plan only about twenty-six per cent of the possible customers failed to purchase within six months' time.

This increase in sales was due to the correct analysis of the distribution of the goods. The problem of the manufacturer was approached from an outsider's viewpoint. The manufacturer hadn't considered this weak link in this hard forged chain before. He didn't enthuse over it until tangible results proved it right.

In another case, a manufacturer found it difficult to market a product which sold on the strength of technical features of construction. Competition was strong. All manufacturers in that line were selling under the same plan. It was this manufacturer's experience that his product could not be sold by direct mail for certain reasons. He was anxious to consider a plan which could be devised that would permit a larger volume of sales through the sales force.

A plan was worked out which not only assisted his salesmen in building up a volume of business, and in cutting the selling costs, but that brought inquiries by mail, giving them specifications which up to that time could not be secured through personal interviews.

A series of tests were made. The tests demonstrated that this manufacturer could actually sell his product in carload lots by mail. Immediate results were satisfactory. The plan, after a thirteen months' test, has proved the means of disposing of the output of two factories.

In another case, a St. Louis manufacturer brought a mail order problem to us. It was a difficult situation, but we found the key to increase sales in a place where he never even looked. We found that eighty-seven per cent of his business was coming from certain localities, fifty-two per cent of his sales territory was not productive. The non-productive territory was eliminated and increased pressure was brought on selected parts of the productive list. As a result his business increased greatly within a few months' time.

Based on right fundamentals, merchandising drives are successful.

Money should not be spent in advertising; IT SHOULD BE INVESTED. The first consideration in any advertising or sales promotion campaign is to properly analyze the sales conditions, take a sales inventory of the market, and build a structure of forceful appeal based on the facts.

The analysis should determine precisely who should be reached, what their viewpoint is, what their purchasing power is, how to reach them in the most effective way.

Selling Problem Vitally Important to Every Manufacturer

It is quite natural that as a class no body or group of men is giving more consideration to economics than manufacturers, especially in recent years when manufacturers by producing goods on a large scale, have reduced the original costs, only to be confronted with the fact that the ultimate price to the consumer has not been correspondingly reduced. This placed all engaged in handling merchandise in somewhat of a false position for they were charging as much for goods produced more cheaply on a quantity basis almost as when they had been produced by more expensive methods.

The reason for this as was explained in the opening chapter, is the increasing cost of transportation, the higher freight rates, the higher rental space paid by retailers, the middlemen's profits, and the added cost of doing business owing to increased wages and other factors of distribution which have affected the rising tide of prices.

It is only natural that under these conditions many manufacturers who have been paying a jobber's commission and a commission to retailers should seek some way of solving the problem of getting their goods into the consumer's hands at the lowest possible rate. To accomplish this objective, many have thought to do away with the wholesale house, and to establish dealer connections direct.

This book does not concern itself with the question of whether this is good or bad policy on the part of the manufacturer, but we have a great deal to say as to the methods used by any manufacturer who decides on this course as his best business policy, for if he uses expensive methods of distribution he has effected no saving, but only made his condition worse by undertaking the details which the jobber previously looked after.

If, on the other hand, the manufacturer adopts a merchandising policy which is sound economically, then he will find his business benefited, and his volume of orders increased.

Solving the Problem of the Manufacturer Who Has a Good Product

The manufacturing concern which has devoted many years of preparation and large sums of money in the perfecting of equipment for the production of an article of unusual merit, is entitled to have the proper sales representation.

Most of the manufacturers who come to us for assistance are men of this kind, who have an article of known merit whose value to the ultimate consumer has been repeatedly proved but whose sales representation is not giving them satisfaction. In every case the correct solution is a matter for the consideration of a merchandiser who has the faculty of making accurate market analyses.

In cases where the articles are staples,

selling to dealers, it is often customary for the manufacturer to market his product through the established selling connections of the wholesaler and the manufacturer's agent. In fact, the majority of successful sales are built up in this way because the wholesaler, devoting all his energy to pushing merchandise, is alive to the market situation much more thoroughly than a manufacturer who would attempt to do his own selling in a desultory way, and he is better prepared to pass on the credit problems of retailers.

In some cases, the product can be sold directly to the consumer, by direct mail methods, and in other cases the product can be most effectively sold through dealers.

Take the case of a concern manufacturing an extract used by tanners. The total list of tanners in the United States is about 700, and all of these tanners can be reached direct by mail; thus the article can be introduced at very small expense. In many instances it is most advantageous to market products through the jobber because the jobber can combine a number of articles and merchandise them at less expense than the manufacturer could merchandise the single articles independently.

There is another advantage in dealing through the wholesale house because the habit of many retail stores prompts them to keep a want list on hand and from this want list the orders are sent to one house so as to save bother in ordering, and also to save the expense of additional freight rates and the trouble and expense of added correspondence.

In many instances, however, it has been found advantageous to market the product of the manufacturer direct to dealers, and where a manufacturer wishes to identify a trade-marked product in the mind of the proprietor of the retail store, he can make the sale himself more advantageously than to trust to a wholesale house.

How to Locate Live Dealers

The safest business course for any manufacturer is to sell to a sufficiently large number of people so that any one or any small combination of his buyers, should they elect to establish their own factory, would not seriously handicap the business.

Many manufacturers, seeing this condition, seek to sell direct to dealers, and where they have an article which sells for a fairly large price — enough to make the dealer see a real reason for separating his article from the bulk order he sends in to the jobber — this is a wise policy because it establishes a source of independent direct retailer demand aside from that of a few wholesalers.

The object of every salesman for a wholesale house, and every salesman for a manufacturer, who is desiring dealer connections, is the livest retail distributor in each town. The most desirable representation the manufacturer or wholesaler can secure is the dealer who will most actively and profitably push the line. In this connection merchandising by mail is the logical medium. Whereas the personal representative seeking dealer connections will spend an average of fifty to one hundred dollars in convincing each dealer of the desirability of taking up his line, direct mail methods have secured dealer representation at a fraction of this cost.

A notable example is a large rug manufacturer in the East who had been advertising in national magazines and securing dealer representation by means of personal solicitors, calling only on the dealers in the large towns.

In looking over the field, it was noted that there were thousands of dealers located in smaller towns who should have been handling the line.

A campaign by mail was instituted which resulted in nearly ten thousand new dealers at a cost of less than $7.00 per dealer, whereas previously the cost had been over $40.00.

The retailer who is interested in direct mail advertising, who reads the advertisements which come to him through the mail is the one who is up on his toes, looking for new opportunities.

The old conservative, slow-going, " satisfied-with-the-old-rut " type of merchant who says, " Oh, it's only an advertisement " is not of much use as a representative to manufacturers or wholesalers. It's the live fellow who is keen to the value of advertising and keen to opportunities who will make the live representative to push your line. That is why merchandising by mail is one of the most satisfactory ways of forming dealer connections.

How Dealers Are Kept on Their Toes

Like every other event in human life, merchandising is of greatest interest when it is first tried. The new book, the new play, the new dress, are all wonderfully interesting. The new broom is applied with vigor, and the new automobile is out on the boulevards every night.

But when the newness has lost its glamour, and that which was unique has become an everyday occurrence, the interest lags, the enthusiasm is gone, and the pep and ginger once exhibited are conspicuous by their absence.

For this natural and very human reason, it is difficult to keep dealers interested and enthusiastically pushing any line, unless the advertising and the sales manager keep alive the enthusiasm that was instilled by the salesman when he first introduced the line to the dealer, the benefits of the merchandising plan will soon be lost and only a fraction of the possible advantages be retained.

Keeping the dealers enthusiastic, making them alive to their opportunities, is one of the most important functions of merchandising through the mail.

All the enthusiasm, pep, and ginger that your best men on the sales force and in the advertising department can muster should be reiterated monthly or more often in messages of help and encouragement sent to the dealers, who are your partners in merchandising your wares.

A bulletin sent out regularly, stories of human interest, window displays, and other types of sales helps — varying with the type of merchandise and the type of dealer — are being used effectively by manufacturers to keep their goods before the public and to make dealers alive to their opportunities for pushing the particular article the manufacturer has produced.

How the Goodwill of Dealers Stimulates Sales

Even though there is nothing of a particularly " peppy " nature to be told to the dealer, even though there are no stories of golden opportunities immediately at hand, no tales of wonderful success by enthusiastic dealers, still the activity of dealers in your behalf can be maintained by messages of goodwill.

The grocer who has been sold on the value of Quaker Oats and who has always received good merchandise whenever he has handled Quaker Oats, and who from time to time has received goodwill messages about Quaker Oats will develop into a Quaker Oats " fan." Almost unknowingly he will give pride of position to the Quaker Oats display and will place the merchandise for which he has the goodwill feeling in the most prominent position.

A good example of the turnover power of an advertised product in comparison with one that is slightly advertised is drawn from a test conducted in Chicago by a group of retail stores. This test covered a period of nine months and its purpose was to establish the consumer's preference, with the sales clerks maintaining an absolutely neutral attitude.

The articles chosen for the test were Aunt Jemima's Pancake Flour, which is heavily advertised, and three other brands of pancake flour which are slightly advertised.

All brands were given equal prominence on the store shelves. They were placed side by side. So far as the stores themselves were concerned, no one brand was pushed beyond another in any manner. The clerks simply waited for the customers to indicate their preference and then tabulated the results. Here they are for the groups of stores covering the nine months' period:

	Cases Sold	Percent
Aunt Jemima's Pancake Flour	735	72½
Slightly advertised Brand # 1	150	15
" " " # 2	75	7½
" " " # 3	50	5

The character of the case was the same for each brand, thirty-six packages to the case.

Many stories could be told of instances where the merchandise of certain manufacturers had been neglected because the manufacturer thought he had done his part when he had produced the article and had introduced it to the dealer. After that he forgot that the dealer, who had had no knowledge of the skill displayed in the manufacturing of the article, or of the struggle that the manufacturer had had in producing this need of mankind, could not be expected to have any enthusiasm about the article which had simply been foisted upon him with instructions to sell it.

Interesting cases could be cited of how a little human sympathy established between the manufacturer and the dealer gave the distributor a definite interest in the goods and created goodwill which at once resulted in an abundant harvest of sales for both.

Manufacturers have become better merchants by using mail methods of marketing to sell in three ways, through jobbers, through agents, through dealers.

In some fields, there are thousands of manufacturers' representatives, many of whom issue catalogs, and all of these representatives can be reached by the appropriate type of mailing pieces which show the merit of the merchandise, and its salability.

This type of presentation once saved the life of an important factory. This factory was manufacturing an article for the order of a mail order house. Because they had this large volume of business from the mail order house, they did not deem it necessary to make any further sales effort, but one morning, after putting about a million dollars into equipment and spending years perfecting the device itself, they received information from the mail order house that after a certain date this mail order house would make the product itself in its own factory, and that their goods would no longer be wanted.

There is a lesson in this example for every manufacturer — a lesson which should show the folly of entrusting all the sales to one individual or firm or group of buyers because whoever has the sales right to your goods has the right to dictate whether or not you shall remain in business. This manufacturer, who had borrowed heavily, was facing great financial difficulties when he came to ask for advice.

An analysis of the field showed that there were 1169 jobbers handling similar devices and the presentation was made to these jobbers which resulted in a volume of business which enabled the manufacturer to weather the tide and to build up new merchandising connections.

One of the common quests of manufacturers is for some large wholesaler who can take care of all of their product. They think that by making this one sale they can avoid trouble and simplify selling, but the great danger is this, that if the wholesaler is taking all of the product of a factory he will eventually grow jealous of the manufacturer's profits and establish his own factory to take care of this extensive line.

Chapter VI

OPENING NEW TERRITORY AND INCREASING SALES FOR JOB-BERS AND RETAILERS

ANY business house which is not aggressively seeking new accounts is on the way to the graveyard. Their old customers die, go out of business and fall away for various reasons. In a few years, with no new accounts added, any business must pass away.

A prominent wholesale house which thought it had been aggressively pushing for new customers, wondered why, in spite of the addition of a large number of new customers each year, the total volume of business was not greatly increased.

An analysis showed that eighteen per cent of their customers fail to renew in the following year. This means that they have to push eighteen per cent ahead in order to keep from slipping back.

Further analysis indicated that salesmen called in towns where the population supported good sized stores. Towns with a population under 3,000 and those not readily accessible were overlooked because personal calls were unprofitable. A sales inventory showed that business was secured from but a small percentage of the possibilities.

The table of population statistics on Page 106 shows that out of a total of 131,809 towns in the United States 129,229 are towns of less than 3000 population, while only 2580 towns have a population of 3000 or more. Very few salesmen will call in towns of less than 3000, so that the merchant who does not do his merchandising by mail loses all the business that comes from the 129,229 towns which are too small for the salesmen to call on.

A plan was developed whereby nearly one hundred per cent of this territory was regularly solicited for business by direct mail advertising.

The plan was followed, methods perfected, and today, this jobber, typical of many others, is securing far more business at a more satisfactory cost of selling.

Keen competition among merchandising houses has developed the science of marketing to the point where the standards of a few years ago would be hopeless today.

Before any accurate system of accounting had been installed by wholesale houses, the general plan followed was to send out salesmen with a full line of samples, who had instructions to call on all of the stores enroute.

With every call the salesmen made, the house received a railroad bill, a list of expenses, and a hotel bill, in addition to paying the drawing account and commission.

It was found that some of the best salesmen were not selling in all of the towns, and the reason for this, when investigated, proved a very sound economic reason — the orders received from some of the small stores were not sufficient to even justify the salesman spending his time making the stop. He could earn more money and send in a larger volume of orders by calling only on those towns and those stores which gave a fairly large volume of orders.

If this were true in the case of the salesman who had only his commission to consider, how much more was it economically true of the house, who had not only to consider the

Why Salesmen Miss a Vast Amount of Potential Business

TABLE SHOWING NUMBER OF TOWNS IN THE U.S.

STATES	Population by States	Towns under 1,000 Pop.	Towns bet. 1,000 and 2,000 Pop.	Towns bet. 2,000 and 3,000 Pop.	Towns bet. 3,000 and 5,000 Pop.	Towns bet. 5,000 and 10,000 Pop.	Towns bet. 10,000 and 25,000 Pop.	Towns bet. 25,000 and 50,000 Pop.	Towns bet. 50,000 and 100,000 Pop.	Towns over 100,000 Pop.
Alabama	2,348,174	3,618	58	26	18	8	7	1	1	1
Arizona	334,162	725	17	7	7	6	1	1		
Arkansas	1,752,204	3,078	45	29	15	8	4	1	1	
California	3,426,861	5,076	101	46	40	26	13	5	4	3
Colorado	939,629	2,489	36	13	9	5	3	2		1
Connecticut	1,380,631	589	66	23	27	7	9	4	2	3
Delaware	223,003	216	5	5	2					1
D. C.	437,571	34		6	1					1
Florida	968,470	2,281	41	17	10	11	2	2	2	
Georgia	2,895,832	3,345	72	34	21	14	7	1	3	1
Idaho	431,866	1,163	20	10	6	7	2			
Illinois	6,485,280	4,007	215	73	50	47	27	12	4	1
Indiana	2,930,390	2,131	97	26	30	23	19	6	5	1
Iowa	2,404,021	2,244	111	36	31	18	11	4	2	1
Kansas	1,769,257	2,201	71	26	29	10	14		2	1
Kentucky	2,416,630	5,252	56	19	24	14	4	2	1	1
Louisiana	1,798,509	3,039	53	17	15	8	4	1		1
Maine	768,014	1,729	119	35	20	11	5	2	1	
Maryland	1,449,661	1,828	40	9	11	3	2	2		1
Massachusetts	3,852,356	1,155	130	69	45	47	39	14	6	7
Michigan	3,668,412	3,600	104	37	24	32	14	9	3	2
Minnesota	2,387,125	2,758	85	33	21	16	8		1	2

	Population									
Mississippi	1,790,618	2,985	46	17	10	8	9			
Missouri	3,404,055	4,095	98	35	28	16	8	2	1	2
Montana	548,889	1,796	21	7	3	6	5	1	1	1
Nebraska	1,296,372	1,395	65	22	8	9	3			
Nevada	77,407	572	13	5	2		1			
New Hampshire	443,083	677	58	17	8	6	6	1	1	
New Jersey	3,155,900	1,368	103	49	41	35	18	10	6	5
New Mexico	360,350	994	20	7	10	3	1			7
New York	10,385,227	4,762	164	70	62	30	36	11	5	
North Carolina	2,559,123	3,788	83	30	14	13	10	4		7
North Dakota	646,872	1,263	28	2	5	3	3			
Ohio	5,759,394	4,951	143	37	48	44	29	12	2	1
Oklahoma	2,028,283	2,151	76	40	21	15	9	1	2	4
Oregon	783,389	2,044	27	7	8	8	3			1
Pennsylvania	8,720,017	8,764	300	134	108	93	57	7	9	
Rhode Island	604,397	215	22	11	17	8	6	3	1	
South Carolina	1,683,724	1,990	49	21	17	8	4	1	1	2
South Dakota	636,547	978	35	6	4	6	1	1		4
Tennessee	2,337,885	4,116	47	24	22	7	3		2	1
Texas	4,663,228	5,758	194	55	48	29	20	5	1	
Utah	449,396	891	42	14	8	2	1	1		2
Vermont	352,428	556	63	4	6	6	3			2
Virginia	2,309,187	5,144	61	14	13	9	5	3	2	
Washington	1,356,621	2,763	41	12	12	7	5	2	1	2
West Virginia	1,463,701	4,019	66	17	13	6	6	2	2	2
Wisconsin	2,632,067	2,555	83	24	32	20	12	7	1	
Wyoming	194,402	652	18	7	2	3	2			1
Total	105,710,620	124,437	3,508	1,284	1,026	721	461	143	76	69

Total towns of less than 3000 population, 129,229. Towns of more than 3000 population, 2580.

amount of the profit they made on the order, but the amount of the saving in railroad, hotel and expense bills!

As a result of this very natural policy of catering to stores in the larger towns only, the smaller merchant was neglected.

This neglect on the part of the salesman is in a large measure responsible for the house supplementing its personal selling by the regular employment of a marketing by mail plan, thereby increasing its annual volume of business.

So it is evident that unless dealers are reached by mail persistently no wholesaler or jobber can possibly get full returns from them. There is great economic waste in the old method of distribution. Smaller towns are not covered at all. The less important and " out of the way " merchants in the towns covered will be slighted or overlooked. This will be reflected in sacrificed business.

A recent instance which illustrates this factor is the case of a large Eastern rug manufacturer. Their product was well advertised nationally. The large cities had been thoroughly canvassed and they had dealers in all these cities enjoying a splendid volume of business, but they still felt that they were not getting anything like the volume of business their expenditure in National advertising entitled them to.

An analysis showed that a tremendous field for possible sales had been absolutely neglected — the small town retailer. A test of the possibilities was made in the Middle and South Atlantic States. A campaign by mail to the small towns in this section sold $73,000 worth of rugs in less than a month. This plan of merchandising has already added over 25,000 dealers to their books.

Gradually manufacturers have learned from experience how practical, simple, and effective the practice of selling by mail has been in completely covering the sales territory. Increases in use of direct selling methods have been the result.

The advent of the motor car has made a tremendous difference in retail buying conditions, especially in the country. The automobile has shortened distances. Where formerly the farmer's wife did her buying almost entirely at the nearest crossroads store, today she goes across the country to take advantage of the larger assortments of stocks and better service of a more progressive retail store.

By bringing people face to face with advanced ideas the automobile has completed a work of tremendous education, and increased the buying tendency vastly.

This combination of favorable conditions has made it possible for some retailers in cities of 3000 population and less to do business of $400,000 or more a year. Without the aid of the motor car for purchasing and for deliveries and the direct mail solicitation of business, these tremendous successes would not have been possible.

Wholesalers awakened to their opportunities of doing business with big stores in small and out-of-the-way locations. They added to the efforts of their salesmen regular mailing pieces containing their offers of merchandise.

Two results were immediately noticeable. One was that the volume of sales from all of the merchants buying their wares showed an increase. This was due to the fact that instead of receiving one call in six weeks or two months from a salesman, the merchant would receive sales presentation from the house every week or ten days.

The other effect was to add to the list of retailers buying from the local house the names of those concerns who previously had been neglected by the personal salesman because they were located in stores which were too out of the way to reach on an economic basis.

How the Stimulus of the Sales Call Changes Indifference to Enthusiasm

And so the plan of keeping in touch with dealers in a very personal way by using " salesmanship through the mail " came to be adopted and applied with a degree of skill which has worked wonders in building up and strengthening the business of the wholesaler.

One wholesaler in Chicago, who does a nation-wide business, adopted the following plan: They sent out to the dealers, who bought from them, and also to those whom they would like to have buy from them, an invitation to come in and see their exhibit rooms, where the goods were displayed.

This invitation was responded to by about one-fourth of the retail dealers to whom it had been addressed.

As a result of the visit to the exhibit rooms, where the tremendous stock was laid out in appropriate display, so many dealers were

FIVE STEPS IN DEALER INTEREST

1. MAIL	2. CALL	3. MAKE FRIENDS	4. SELL	5. GOODWILL
1. Mail advertising matter direct to dealers.	1. Before calling on the dealer: a. Find out who his principal competitors are. b. What brands his competitors sell. c. Learn if he pushes sales or not. d. What brand (or brands) he sells or pushes. e. Note his window display and space used by same. f. Learn something about his way of doing business (i.e., whether he likes high-grade merchandise; whether he advertises, etc.) 2. Upon meeting him:	1. Induce him to talk by being frank and honest with him. Have him answer questions of things you would like to know about. 2. Tell him what you can do for him in a fairly definite way. 3. Learn about these points: a. What volume he sells. b. Whether manufacturers he is now buying from co-operate with him closely: 1. By advertising in newspapers, on billboards, etc. 2. By direct-by-mail	1. Show why your line is better. a. Tell about material and workmanship *briefly.* 2. Explain how the dealer's sales will increase by selling it. a. How he can tie up with your advertising. b. How he can cash in on the demand you have created and which will be filled by someone. Why not him? c. Explain your sales promotion plans. Exhibit portfolio showing what you do. d. How his sales will	1. Don't overstock the dealer. Sell him something that will make quick turnover. 2. Give prompt attention to orders and make all shipments accurate. 3. Send through the mails pointers which will help him speed up sales. 4. Maintain a spirit of friendly helpfulness at all times. 5. Don't let an inhuman and cold credit department destroy the friendship.
2. Support this with trade paper, billboard and newspaper advertising.				
3. Send personal letters to all prospective dealers. Tell them about a new dealer you have just sold; of some unusual testimonial letter; of anything that will interest them.				
4. Send postal cards telling dealers of all the other sales you are making in their vicinity.				

5. Send one or two advance cards telling dealer you have a proposition which is sure to interest him.

a. Be perfectly natural.
b. Be confident and unafraid.
c. Be earnest.
d. Tell him you are there to help him in his sales work.
e. State your name and company.
f. Start by making some statement which will be of interest to him.

efforts.
3. By window displays.
4. By helping him sell large users.
5. By helping him conduct special selling events.

4 Put yourself in position to show dealer why he should take on your line.

increase because of more customers being brought in.
e. Show how his reputation can be increased by handling a well-known line everyone admits is standard.

3. Explain why he will have no difficulty in making sales. Consumer resistance is largely broken down by publicity.

4. Exhibit testimonial letters to clinch your arguments and to bear out your statements.

5. Review points you have previously learned about his business and turn them to your advantage.

6. Mail new window displays, signs, etc., frequently.

Mail methods are an important link between dealer and manufacturer enthused with the possibilities of the line they were handling that the orders from this twenty-five per cent were more than doubled. The actual sales from these same dealers during the ensuing six months increased over two hundred per cent.

One of the defects of personal selling, which is hard to overcome, is that the personal salesman follows the line of least resistance. When he goes into a store he knows that the buyer has previously bought leather goods and novelties from him. It is very natural, therefore, that his approach is along the line where resistance has been broken down — leather goods and novelties. This is especially true of the commission salesmen, who prefer quick sales to doing missionary work.

By the time he has signed the order for these lines, he is pretty well satisfied with himself and goes on his way. The habit has been established where this particular buyer looks on your house as being one from which to purchase pocketbooks, handkerchiefs and gloves.

With the mail-selling method, however, this limitation in presenting the line is eliminated. The direct mail literature and catalog which present the illustrations and talking points for all of the articles the house has in stock is in nearly every instance, a revelation even to those people with whom a concern has been doing business for a long time because but a small percentage have ever been sold on complete line by any of the personal salesmen.

It is coming to be recognized as a very potent factor that the wholesaler's best opportunity for business is right with the people to whom he is selling a part of his line — to get them to buy the other things which he carries.

The wholesaler who is continually adding new lines, should see that the trade which buys from him is regularly informed as to the full line of articles he carries. He should make efforts to sell not only the line he is selling to the particular dealer, but to sell the lines which that dealer is not buying.

The opportunity for the wholesaler to increase his volume of business at a fraction of his present selling costs has been clearly demonstrated by the application of mail marketing methods not only by concerns doing a wholesale business entirely by mail, but to a more or less important degree by a considerable per cent of wholesalers whose usual channels of sales are through salesmen.

Retailers Sell in Rural Districts By Using Mail Selling Methods

A salesman out in an Iowa town called on a storekeeper who had an old-fashioned store in a splendid location.

The salesman was of a creative type and was urging the storekeeper to change his methods, and to adopt newer selling ideas. The reply of the storekeeper was: " Oh, these old methods were good enough for my father and I guess they're good enough for me." The salesman answered, and he could make this answer because of his experience and familiarity with the situation: " Your father when he established this store, was the most progressive merchant of his time, that's why he won success. If he had been content with the methods of your grandfather, he would never have established any type of business at all. He never refused to consider new ideas, and adopted the things that had proved successful with other merchants. If he were alive he would be the first one to recognize that the community your store is serving is greatly changed today, and that you must adopt changed methods to take advantage of these changed conditions."

That's the whole story in a nutshell. Business which rightfully belongs to the local retailer is going to the cities, the " strong " country town stores, and to the mail order houses — why? The only answer is that business goes where it is invited.

Someone has made the remark that " business is sensitive — it goes only where it is invited, and stays only where it is well treated." If the mail order house is sending out invitations to the trade, and is not following definite plans to offset it through advertising, it is easy to figure out where business will be sacrificed.

Within a few blocks of almost any retail store are people who seldom pass the shop windows. Their interest leads them in other directions. They will seldom know the beauty of the goods you have displayed unless you place the sales information before them by advertising. In the daily mail they will receive from mail order houses beautifully illustrated catalogs, showing the women in the houschold the latest styles in dresses, the new and fascinating ideas that have been created by Dame Fashion, and hundreds of things needed which they can easily order by mail.

In the Sunday papers they will see the advertisements of the stores in the big city, and of progressive local competitors, showing attractive merchandise often at exceptional prices, and the natural result is a desire to visit the big city, and do some shopping in progressive stores where these desirable things are so easily obtainable.

From the local retailer, who is the logical one to receive that trade, they hardly ever receive anything to excite their interest, no evidence of goods, service, or ability to take care of their needs and desires.

If this is true in regard to the people who live just a few blocks away from any retailer, it is doubly true in regard to those who live in the rural districts. These people visit a town possibly only once a month and even if they visit town and pass a store they may not see the goods displayed in the window. These are but a small part of your stock. Even if they come into the store and make a purchase they see only the articles in that section. Possibly some things which they could be induced to desire are hidden away from their view in some obscure corner of the room.

The situation is different, however, with newspaper or direct by mail advertising, suggesting timely articles for their consideration, and drawing attention to the store as their local trading center, also pointing out that the values are just as great or even greater in the merchandise. The local retailer has a distinct advantage in this respect.

It is natural for people to trade at stores that are easily accessible and to which they can go personally and inspect the goods instead of trading with people at a distance where they have to wait for some days for service and cannot inspect the purchase until they have paid for it. The retailer has an opportunity to cultivate his territory, and how this opportunity can be developed is demonstrated by the remarkable success of those stores which have seen the light, and gone after their local territory with a campaign of marketing by mail.

When we read of merchants, who in stores of small dimensions have built businesses of $400,000 a year in towns of only a few hundred people, by cultivating the trade in the rural territory, we know the immensity of the possibilities for the retailer who will apply as much intelligence to the development of the trade in his territory as he does in renting his store, to buying his goods, and hiring his salespeople, and to his store salesmanship.

There is growing throughout the United States a movement on the part of retailers to go after business more aggressively, and to counteract the inroads of the city stores and the mail order houses. There is a real desire on the part of these retailers who have awakened to their opportunities to build up their business in a large way.

In fact the retailer is being forced to adopt more aggressive selling methods. He can no longer be a mere storekeeper. The inroads of the chain store, with its " cash and carry " policy makes it imperative that the retail merchant become active in building up the real possibilities of his business.

The last forty years have seen the activity now designated as the " chain store " grow from a negligible, unrespected way of doing business to one of the most important in the whole range of trade. There are now in the United States not less than 50,000 chain grocery store units.

How Retailers Welcome the Coöperation of Wholesalers and Manufacturers

This desire on the part of the retailers to do more aggressive advertising, and to show themselves real merchants in their territories is evidenced by the increasing response received to the efforts of wholesalers and manufacturers who have offered their services in coöperating with the dealers to better their advertising methods.

A few years ago the offer of the manufacturer to supply window trim, circulars for distribution, electrotypes for newspaper display, moving picture films, and other advertising accessories was looked upon with an " I can't be bothered " attitude, and the response was very meager.

But recent experiences are showing that those progressive retailers who did accept the practical sales helps offered, and intelligently coöperated, have had such remarkable results that others, formerly indifferent, are gladly following in their footsteps.

In talking with a retail furniture man he commented on some advertising recently mailed out by a manufacturer which had lost its point of contact because no local dealer's

Co-Operation Pays

Relative Costs of Selling

Taken from analysis of methods of two firms in the hardware specialty trade.

WHERE RETAILER PLANNED AND PAID FOR ALL ADVERTISING	WHERE MANUFACTURER CO-OPERATED BY PROVIDING ADVERTISING AT COST
Volume of Business Resulting **$5870**	**Volume of Business Resulting** **$8890**
Cost of Advertising **$1130** Done by 12 Retailers	Cost of Advertising **$1020** Done by 10 Retailers

The same cost to dealers provided double the quantity of circulars and also provided posters, electros, and window cards. The quality of design and color, however, was mainly responsible for the larger returns.

name appeared. He said: "If manufacturers would supply us with advertising of this type, with space for our own imprints, we would be glad to supply the list of prospects free, to furnish the postage, and frequently, in addition, to pay a reasonable portion of the production cost."

This spirit contrasts with the experience of people who tried very hard a few years ago to induce dealers to use mailing pieces, and found that they were not even willing to pay for postage, and frequently when advertising was supplied to them, it would be allowed to lie under the counter, or to be thrown down in the basement with the rubbish.

The Basis of Dealer Coöperation

We have one account that runs into thousands of pieces every day, where the dealer furnishes the names, pays the postage, and the cost of the addressing. The coöperation of the manufacturer by buying this printing in large quantities enables every dealer to put out exceptional advertising at small cost, and this is welcomed by hundreds of live, aggressive dealers.

In fact, this concern will not let any dealer handle its line unless a contract is made providing for the carrying out of the advertising program. This provision is made and insisted on because it is recognized that only through carrying out the plans completely and systematically can the best results be secured.

Another concern manufacturing clothing arranges with the dealer to furnish the cost of the postage and one half of the printing cost. The dealers have coöperated with this service in a satisfactory way after being sold on the benefits that would result.

Quite a number of wholesalers and manufacturers provide printed matter free which the dealers use, either having the literature passed out by boys or mailing to their prospects.

The most satisfactory way of handling this is to have the dealer supply his list of names so that immediately a new line comes in, the lists throughout the country are circularized simultaneously in an organized way, either in the advertising department of the firm or by using the services of a responsible mail service organization.

A test made by the manufacturer of a line of agricultural implements showed that dealers who used the manufacturers' plan of co-operating in aggressive local advertising, sold approximately three times the volume of sales that an equal number of non-coöperating dealers are sold. The data on this test is typical of that of other tests.

A wholesaler of general merchandise has found that dealers who advertise regularly with a definite plan behind it do a bigger business, make better profit, establish better goodwill, and repeat year after year far better than do retailers who confine their advertising to spasmodic efforts, who fail to take advantage of the coöperation of manufacturers, and who do not conduct their advertising in the same efficient, systematic manner in which they do their personal sales efforts.

The lesson in these facts must be apparent to every person who studies the merchandising problem. An evolution is taking place which is for the betterment of business.

The business of the future will continue to be done in the largest measure by the group which has always led in selling — the manufacturer will sell his product to the wholesaler, the wholesaler will sell to the retailer, and the retailer to the consumer.

But the aggressive policies of the mail order house and the chain store have shown to all these three units in the sale the necessity for more thorough merchandising. Each must recognize their mutuality of interest with the others and by coöperation profit from the performance of helpful service.

The manufacturer must not be content to unload on the wholesaler and the wholesaler to unload on the retailer. They must be concerned right up to the time the goods reach the consumer. Stores which exist to sell goods must not be neglected. Their sales potentiality must be cultivated, and the development of all of these ideas can come through only one channel — the more extensive practice of merchandising by mail.

CHAPTER VII

HOW THE MAILS ARE USED TO STRENGTHEN THE HANDS OF THE SALES FORCE

One of the most tremendous opportunities for the postage stamp is its use in helping salesmen to become more efficient.

Why is it that salesmen are subject to greater turnover than any other class of individuals?

One authority says that salesmen divide themselves into three classes, those coming in, those going out, and those sticking to their job.

He further states that if a hundred salesmen are sent out thirty per cent of them will immediately begin producing business, fifty per cent will begin to write back, " Our competitors have more up-to-date styles. Our prices are too high, etc." The other twenty per cent will be miserable failures.

Does any business man tolerate this percentage of inefficiency in other departments of his business?

When we analyze the cause of this tremendous turnover in the sales force, and the reason for such a high percentage of failure, we find it is very largely because of the lack of direct mail support.

There is nothing more discouraging than to be sent out to interview a keen, hard-headed business man — to be forced to fight for the privilege of an interview — to fight against prejudice — and finally find that you have been talking to a man who is not actually a prospect.

One of the greatest wastes in selling is the time which must be employed by the salesman doing unnecessary things. The salesman calls on a business house, and finds the man he wants to interview is not in. When he returns again he finds that the man is in conference, and after probably waiting a half a day, he finally obtains an interview, but then only under unfavorable conditions.

Compare this with the man whose visit has been announced ahead of time. He comes in to a definitely stated appointment, as the representative of a known company on a specified subject and receives the undivided attention of the individual whom he calls on.

Is it any wonder that under the first named system — calling on cold leads — that the salesman becomes quickly discouraged? He finds it hard to sell. His volume of business is small, and prospects ahead of him do not look very alluring. Under these conditions, it is hardly to be expected that any large percentage of men will continue on a sales force.

When we analyze the reasons for only thirty per cent of salesmen actually delivering orders, we find that the human element enters into it. Out of every hundred men, only a limited number can grasp and understand your project, and present it in a masterly way. Other men on your sales force are more or less apologetic and half-hearted in their presentation, and fail utterly to grasp the significance and purpose of your business.

So when you rely solely on personal representation, your product is presented to prospects according to these human frailties. A certain percentage of the people called on will receive a good strong message and be sold on the value of your product but the great majority of them will receive only a weak presentation of its merits.

On the other hand, your best merchandising story is told where you use modern mail methods. You employ one strong, powerful merchandiser with a keen analytical mind — and in this way present the facts as convincingly to all your prospects as your best salesman would present them. With this strong, thorough presentation of your product as the introduction there is no occasion for any salesman to be apologetic. Knowing the type of presentation that has been made, he walks in with a feeling of confidence and in a far greater number of cases, is successful in " landing the order."

To illustrate how direct mail methods help the salesman the following example is cited:

You employ a hundred salesmen and the volume of business is $2,000,000 a year. Total selling expense is $600,000 a year or thirty per cent. The average sales expense in your line is twenty-one per cent, showing that your selling costs are entirely too high.

A rival concern, which also employs a hundred salesmen, does a business of $4,000,-000 each year and their selling costs are $750,-

000. The difference in your selling methods is merely this, that they spend $50,000 a year in direct mail advertising while you spend nothing. If by adding this $50,000 to your sales expense, you can increase your sales $2,000,000, will it pay?

It might be implied from this question that it is one which should be decided as a matter of financial policy, but as a matter of fact the necessity of adopting the newer methods of selling is even more imperative than dollars and cents. Sooner or later your salesmen are going to learn that the salesmen for the rival concern are making bigger commissions, earning more money than they are in their job with you, and the firm which gives the greatest promise to the salesman — the most positive assurance of higher earnings — will entice your salesmen away from you, and diminish your selling ability. On the other hand, there is little chance of your succeeding in attracting salesmen who have worked for a more successful house, and who have been used to the support of mail methods in boosting their volume of sales.

It becomes almost a matter of necessity for the wholesaler and the manufacturer in these days to adopt a definite mail merchandising policy or suffer serious consequence. It is for this reason that an increasing number of manufacturers and wholesalers are keeping direct mail literature going regularly to the trade as an insurance of goodwill and help for salesmen in their sales efforts.

The Southwest Cracker Company states that, although their salesmen reach half the field once a week and the rest once every two weeks, they have found it pays them to send literature to all customers and prospects regularly each month. They have done this for years and have found that this method of sustaining goodwill has been the backbone of their success.

In spite of fluctuations in sales efforts which result from the hiring of brilliant and mediocre salesmen, direct mail advertising has maintained their high standards and kept the reputation of the firm from lagging at any point in their merchandising appeal.

Let us consider a typical case to illustrate the attitude of many salesmen to advertising helps: Tom Brown was a fairly successful salesman of the old school. When he heard that his firm intended to send out advertising to the prospects he was calling on, he was " peeved." He was antagonistic to the plan of advertising, because he had no clear appreciation of how it could help him. " I don't need any advertising to bolster up my sales. It is just an attempt of the firm to do without salesmen and save our salaries. If they tell the whole story by mail, I won't have an interesting story to tell myself." That's a sample of the confused reasoning that Tom used.

But a little while later, out on the road, he had sold his usual type of order to a customer, and was just about to leave when the customer said: " Oh, by the way, I received a circular from your house. What is this new line of baskets you are putting out?" Tom explained the line — he hadn't thought of mentioning it before — and received quite a substantial addition to his order. When similar things happened several times on his trip, and he got back home, he recognized that he had sold more than 25 per cent above his usual sales volume. Not only that, but while he was away on another trip, quite a volume of new orders came in of their own volition for which Tom received the credit.

Then Tom began to take notice of the advertising pieces, and asked that he be supplied with a copy of each one. The advertising pieces told him things he had never thought of in regard to the merchandise he was selling, and it inspired him to take the initiative so that on the next trip, instead of waiting for the customer to broach the subject, he would say: " Oh, by the way, did you get our circular on the new style pocketbooks? " This time he found his orders increased about 33 per cent. Is it any wonder that now Tom is one of the most enthusiastic boosters for advertising to supplement his efforts?

The High Cost of Sending Salesmen on Cold Leads

A duplicating machine company in Chicago, recently made a survey which established a number of facts which should be thought over by sales managers no matter what line they are selling. Briefly summarized they are as follows:

1 — Allowing for Sundays, legal holidays, Saturday half holidays, two weeks' vacation,

sickness and unavoidable absence from work, totaling altogether about 100 days, there are 265 days of the year that the average salesman is on the job.

2 — Allowing 8 hours as his possible productive time, 8 hours multiplied by 265 days gives 2120 hours per year.

3 — The salesman averages 20 per cent of his full productive time, face-to-face with his prospects. This amounts to 425 hours per year.

4 — 425 hours per year means only 8 hours per week. The balance is absorbed in getting around.

5 — Experience has demonstrated that the salesman makes about six conscientious calls per day. These calls approximate 15 minutes each — 32 calls each week.

6 — About half of the calls made result in real interviews, making 16 interviews per week.

7 — About half of the interviews are "favorable," making 8 calls per week of 15 minutes each, or an average of $1\frac{1}{2}$ hours of worthwhile selling talk face-to-face with prospects per week.

Upon close examination you will find that while these figures are startling, they have a convincing way about them, which brings us to the proposition of either helping the salesman get a higher percentage of favorable interviews out of the calls he makes, or putting on more salesmen to increase business.

Mr. Twist says that a few years ago some tests were made by this same concern to learn why salesmen fell down when it came to closing sales. The results indicated that sixty-five per cent of such failures were almost entirely due to just two factors: either improper first approach, or failure to recognize the psychological moment for closing the sale. "Improper approach" was the bigger factor of the two.

They believe that the function of all good advertising is to "shorten the time and lower the expense of making the actual sale." They therefore decided that direct mail advertising was the medium best suited to act as their junior salesman.

A junior salesman can make approximately 40 calls per week — say 2,000 a year at the outside; and costs about $40.00 per week. This means a cost per call of about $1.00. To this must be added around $1.50 more for traveling expenses when on the road.

At the same expense, direct mail juniors can easily go to a given prospect ten times where the man junior goes once. This means an average of 10 cents per call. Therefore, mail juniors can make 400 calls per week for the same money it takes to have man juniors make 40 calls.

Laboratory tests show that about eighty-five per cent of all knowledge is derived from the sense of sight. Mail juniors can attract and hold the prospect's attention through their graphic appeal, while the man junior must depend largely on the sense of hearing, because he gets his story over orally.

Every salesman who has worked on a proposition where it is necessary for him to go out and dig up his own leads — to make " hit or miss " calls knows that it is impossible to earn big money in this way.

The house to house canvasser, or peddler of small articles is possibly the only type of salesman who today receives no advertising support. Even the Fuller Brush representatives in this field receive what amounts to advertising support — the introduction of a gift of a brush to the housewife with every call they make.

But in consideration of merchandising by mail, we are not particularly interested in methods for house to house solicitations. We want to consider the field for merchandising in a big way — the way in which 80 per cent of all sales are made — the contact between wholesaler and retailer. Calling on a business man unannounced involves an unnecessary waste of time. Sometimes it is impossible to gain an interview. The man whom the salesman should see is engaged in some lengthy conference, he is out of town, or is away on some business mission.

In some lines of trade, such as department stores, where audience with salesmen can be given only a part of each day and long waiting is imperative, the time spent in selling is but a small fraction of the time lost in waiting by the salesman.

A manufacturer of headlights for locomotives found his salesmen forced to spend 75 per cent of their selling time waiting in anterooms. When they were permitted to talk their proposition, the entire preliminary missionary work had to be covered in the interview. The plan of sending a monthly mailing to the list, featuring the advantages of the product, was adopted, with the result that when the men called the proposition had been introduced and the resistance to selling was gradually overcome in a very gratifying way.

When a salesman is asked to wait, he often spends hour after hour sitting on the bench in the outer office waiting for an opportunity to see the business executive. Then when he finally does get the opporunity to see the business executive, the salesman who has been subjected to all of these discouragements is not in a very favorable frame of mind to influence the desires of the business man to want the article he has for sale. The entire work of creating desire as well as selling is forced upon him in an interview that is often brief.

Part of the aversion of business executives to buying from salesmen who call in this way is due to the fact that they know that selling costs are high, and that the actual value they receive in the article itself is not of sufficiently large proportion of the price to justify their considering it a " good buy."

The number of cases where the salesman is asked to " call again," or is told that the executive is " not interested," or is asked to " leave literature " can be reduced through a policy of direct mail advertising.

Increased Percentage of Sales Where Missionary Work Has Been Accomplished Through the Mail

While theories are interesting, the best " provers " are actual figures, and I want to quote some actual figures taken from records of " before and after treatment," where houses have adopted a policy of sending out educative advertising direct to the business executives ahead of the salesman's call.

A salesman for a printing concern, calling on cold leads, sold an average of less than seven per cent of the people called on. The policy of the house changed, and they used mail methods of producing leads. When these leads were handed to the salesmen they succeeded in closing eighty-six per cent of the people called on.

A salesman for a refrigerator company calling on furniture dealers to get them to accept representation for his line called on

THREE METHODS OF SELLING

METROPOLITAN

Personal Calls
Cost-average $7.50

Mail Calls
Cost-average 5¢

Magazine Readers
Cost about 2¢

BALANCED QUOTA

50 % Personal Selling
25 % Direct Mail
25 % Magazine & News

DISTRICT
of 500 mile radius

Personal Calls
Cost-average $25

Mail Calls
Cost-average 5¢

Magazine Readers
Cost about 1¢

BALANCED QUOTA

33 % Personal Selling
33 % Direct Mail
33 % Magazine & News

NATION WIDE

Personal Calls
Cost-average $50

Mail Calls Cost-average 5¢

Magazine Readers
Cost-average ¼¢

BALANCED QUOTA

25 % Personal Selling
33 % Direct Mail
42 % Magazine & News

Above figures are not to be taken as a guide to your business. They represent the method of arriving at a balanced quota as a business, by expansion changes from local to national field.

over four hundred dealers, at a cost of approximately $6000.00 and succeeded in getting forty-two of them to accept representation. After adopting a direct mail schedule of five pieces, which cost $3000, the same salesman went out and called on one hundred twenty interested dealers at a cost of $2600 and succeeded in bringing back acceptances from eighty-five of them.

A salesman for a washing machine company made calls on three hundred sixty prospective dealers at a cost to the firm of $4600, and obtained only eight representatives. Following a direct mail campaign another salesman went out to sixty interested leads at a cost of less than $1000 and signed up forty-three representatives.

Sales managers are sometimes misled in regard to the cost of personal selling because they do not analyze the cost of making each sale.

Some very interesting figures were recently submitted by one aggressive sales manager who had taken the trouble to make this analysis.

A typical salesman was cited. He calls on 300 customers twice a year. His salary is $6,000. His traveling expenses $3500, a total expense of $9500 to make 600 calls. The average of $15.83 per call or $31.66 per year for each customer to whom he sells.

This salesman sells $270,000 a year, an average of $900 to each customer, at a cost to the house of three per cent.

An analysis of the salesman's sales proves that eighty per cent of his sales which amount to $216,000 were made to eighty-four of his customers at a cost to the house of about one and one-quarter per cent and that twenty per cent of his sales were sold to two hundred and sixteen customers, and cost more than ten per cent to sell.

It costs this firm $25,000 to sell $2,000,000.00 worth of merchandise and it costs them $50,-000 to sell $500,000.00 worth.

The remedy is obvious. It lies in dividing up the sales work between men and mail matter. Mail calls can be made at a few cents each, whereas man calls in this case were $15.83.

This sales manager proved the economy of mail merchandising by using salesmen to call only on those prospects whose business could be obtained personally at a cost of four per cent or less. Customers costing more than four per cent to sell were transferred to the mail selling list. The calls by mail cost only a few cents and relieved the salesman of the necessity of making these calls, enabling him to increase his volume of profitable orders.

Thus was an intelligent solution of the high cost of selling worked out by the use of mail selling in place of unprofitable personal calls.

According to the statistics sent in by the insurance companies in the United States, in making their report to the authorities, it is shown that in the year of 1922, the average cost of selling $1000 insurance was $23.10 by companies who sell through salesmen almost exclusively and do only a moderate amount of advertising to support the salesmen.

Some insurance companies do considerable advertising to support their salesmen. The Metropolitan Life Insurance Company of New York is an example of this type. The cost to this company of selling every thousand dollars' worth of insurance in 1922 was $11.63.

The Phoenix Life Insurance Company, through 1700 salesmen, sold $20,000,000 insurance in one year. Analysis showed that the great bulk of this business came from fifteen per cent of the salesmen, and that eighty-five per cent of the salesmen were doing very poor work.

The company worked out a strong sales plan, with literature to be sent to prospects to secure leads. The results of this plan of mail sales support has been that in a later year about 500 salesmen sold $47,135,000 insurance.

A manufacturer of a paper product was able, through letter advertising, to reduce the average number of calls necessary to sell a customer from seven to five. They found that the average cost of a salesman's call was $11.23. Their cost system showed that the cost of a personally dictated letter was fifteen cents. Only three letters were used in the sales followup to support the salesmen. These letters, costing less than a dollar, saved this company $22.46 in non-productive salesmen's calls.

Figures like these tell the story of economic merchandising. They indicate to the sales manager, whose sales costs are running high, a very opportune method of reducing them, a method to which he should give not merely his assent to its adoption, but his earnest study and his enthusiastic coöperation.

It is not in human nature to make large business contracts, or to tie up definitely on a sales policy involving thousands of dollars on some individual's " say-so "; unless missionary work has been done by advertising making him familiar with the advantages of the article merchandised, very little can be accomplished by a one-time call of the salesman.

There are of course " one-call " men but they are very hard to find, and sales managers must work with the material they have.

The Economic Folly of Using a " Closer " For Educative Work

The examples shown previously in this chapter are ample evidence of the economic loss which follows the use of a five thousand dollar man on a two cent job. Where the introduction of an article to a live, aggressive dealer can be accomplished through the mails at a cost of a few cents, it is economic folly to send a high-powered salesman, who must necessarily be paid a high salary to accomplish the same work as the very inexpensive mailing.

Not only is it false economy from the viewpoint of the additional expense of introducing the article, but it is poor economics from the human standpoint because the man of great enthusiasm, the " natural closer," is a man of high ambitions, and to tie him down to doing the primitive work of introducing articles is actually discouragement for him, and does not give full vent to the use of his energy.

In selling higher priced specialties the advantages of direct mail selling is apparent in cutting down the time in making sales and the cost of selling. The Addressograph Company for instance sends a series of seven mailing pieces to prospects before a salesman calls.

The Ditto Company have found by comparison of salesmen's reports that the plan of sending a series of mailing pieces, costing about $2.00, reduces the time required in selling the prospect twenty-five per cent, with consequent saving in selling cost and greater profit to the firm.

To use high-powered salesmen to introduce

articles would be like using the dean of the faculty of a great university to teach the kindergarten class.

True economics will point the way to the use of kindergarten methods for the kindergarten class. It will be more successful for the kindergarten to be taught by a young person who understands the work than by a professor who in most cases would talk over their heads.

The above simile may at first appear to be out of place, but if you will examine methods in detail, you will see that it is not so far fetched because the high-powered salesman — the man of great energy and enthusiasm — is naturally impatient, and he does not do such a good job of educating the business man on an unknown project as the type of man we find in the advertising field — the copywriter, who knows how and who will take the time to analyze an article from the customer's viewpoint and explain it with sufficient detail to make a reasoning man see its real advantage.

For the cost of sending one high-powered salesman to the business man, he can be reached with many pieces of direct mail. If six, ten or twenty pieces of well prepared advertising, directed in a personal way to the attention of the buyer, do not produce a favorable attitude and a genuine desire for the goods on the part of the recipient, then the fault is not with the method but with the article itself, or the price or terms quoted.

Aside from the actual advertising of the features of the articles advertised, the policy of advertising helps the salesman by creating confidence in the house. The policy is well expressed by the Fitzsimmons Company of Youngstown, Ohio: "When our salesman sends in his card he isn't altogether a stranger. He represents a concern whose character is somewhat known from advance advertising. He is selling something besides impersonal metal. Certain ideals of service are back of him — certain standards of doing business. It is those ideals and standards that we try to set forth in our messages to the trade — those things that make this a good concern to do business with."

"Pepping" Up the Sales Force with New Ideas

All advertising and sales work should be correlated. If the advertising department is instructed to sell nails to hardware merchants, and the advertising pieces talk nails and create the desire for nails, then let it be understood by the selling force that they are to coöperate and to talk nails and sell nails when they make their trip.

If, on the other hand, the personal salesman goes out and talks stoves and refrigerators, and doesn't say a word about nails, the connection is lost, and only those dealers who are aggressive enough to remind the salesman about the circular will contribute towards an increased volume of sales.

The sales story of nearly every traveling salesman who travels over the same route carrying a routine message, becomes very monotonous and he loses interest and enthusiasm because of a lack of new ideas — " different " methods that are new and lack the monotony common to old approaches. One of the big functions of the advertising department is to create new ideas, and to enthuse merchants, salesmen, and even the manufacturer himself, with a more aggressive way of looking at their sales problems.

It is easy when there is a centralized department, such as the advertising department can easily be made, to have all the ideas on selling come to this department. Then instead of each salesman working on his own ideas, every one of the one hundred salesmen gives the other ninety-nine the benefit of his experiences on the road. If these are all repeated to the advertising department, new ideas can be sent out to all of the salesmen one hundred times as fast as they could get them in any other way.

We are all familiar with the enthusiasm which can be generated in a selling organization by a talk from the sales manager who calls them into convention. We know that with a man who can handle such a situation right, the salesmen can go out with new vim and energy and accomplish a vastly increased volume of sales. The reason for this is that the new ideas and the enthusiasm assist in producing business. Business is always available. Men are in business to do business, and anything which will help them is welcomed.

The salesman's bulletin issued by many houses is a regular " pep " creator. Records of what the other fellow is doing, contests between salesmen, and hundreds of stimulative sales efforts make a little bulletin of this kind so vitally interesting to the salesmen that they look forward to it as the one bright spot in their week's routine.

There is nothing like an interested and co-operating advertising department to keep the enthusiasm of the salesmen up to the highest point with a regular " pep " producing bulletin.

Building Goodwill For Salesmen

Probably one of the earliest used advertising pieces, coöperating with salesmen, was the " advance card " announcing that " our Mr. Blank will call on you on such and such a date." If in addition to this announcement the firm would tell something about the goods that he would introduce, or about the interesting nature of the service helps he would bring, it would make a wonderful difference in the reception a salesman receives from the business executives. The many variants of this obvious introduction have all aided in creating goodwill for salesmen.

A house magazine sent to dealers and purchasers of large quantities of the goods sold by a wholesaler or manufacturer can be used to build up this goodwill for salesmen.

Quite frequently in magazines of this kind we find news of general interest and talks about the merits of the goods advertised. Also little stories about what the salesmen are doing.

The story of how Tom Jones won the fat men's race at the employes' picnic may not seem of much general interest to the grocer out in Iowa, but if the grocer knows Tom Jones, the chances are the next time Tom Jones calls, the grocer will josh him about it, and in this way a little feeling of human understanding is established.

Through the mail, hundred of ways can be used about telling stories about customers and their methods, and about salesmen and their ways, and so bring them closer together.

CHAPTER VIII

BUILDING THE PRESTIGE OF AN INSTITUTION BY MAIL

The extent to which mail advertising methods can be applied successfully in building the prestige and goodwill of an institution is unlimited. The opportunities were never greater than they are today for every business house to include in its program of sales promotion, a definite plan of building the prestige of the house through the effective use of the mails. Building goodwill means building confidence, and all businesses are permanently founded on confidence, and out of this confidence comes coöperation and success.

One cannot take an inventory of the outstanding successes among great business houses of the country that have effectively used the mails to build prestige for their institution, as well as their products, without putting at the top of the list the NATIONAL CASH REGISTER COMPANY.

154

John H. Patterson who founded the National Cash Register Company, was one of the greatest exponents of mail advertising methods to establish confidence and build institutional goodwill and prestige among his customers, prospects, agents and salesmen. In his intensive mail advertising methods he did regularly what others have only done spasmodically. For example, in his early plan of goodwill and prestige building among his agents he developed *The N. C. R.*, a house organ for passing on ideas and showing sales records — selling quotas based on the opportunities to make sales.

Mr. Patterson proceeded on the principle that a business should not have secrets, but what one agent knew was good for every other agent to know. *The N. C. R.* house organ was established with this very thought in mind — to disseminate information, create goodwill, good feeling and understanding among his agents. That was twenty years or more ago and it has continued uninterrupted ever since. Today's issues are newspaper size.

A similar house organ was started, known as *N. C. R. Storekeeper's News*, and it has continued ever since, going regularly to retail merchants throughout the country, and this direct mail effort throughout a score of years has done more to create goodwill and make for better accounting and storekeeping methods than any other one medium.

Those who know Mr. Patterson well, credit him with these words:

" There are two things in my business to which I devote the greater part of my time — the first is advertising, the second is selling. If we advertise properly we pave the way for our salesmen. If we have a thoroughly trained selling force — the men can sell our goods in good times or bad. The important things to do, therefore, are to improve our advertising and improve our sales force. If we get orders we can easily manufacture the product, but we must first get the orders."

There's a moral in this statement for every business executive.

Too many corporations and firms are prone to leave the advertising and selling end of their business to subordinates, and to look upon advertising as a necessary evil. However, when it comes to utilizing mail methods to create goodwill and prestige that have a cash value — why they are for it possibly for a time. Each year when budgets are made out, and the board or executive committee are passing on them, some lawyer, banker or other inactive member of the board will usually suggest to the president that perhaps this sort of advertising had better be discontinued. The chief executive, not entirely sold on the merits of institutional promotion work by mail, does not raise any strenuous objection and so the plan is sacrificed.

I have found, out of an experience of twenty years in advertising and merchandising, that there are two occasions in nearly every business — particularly in the manufacturing field — when a firm advertises without any unusual amount of coaxing or pressure: " When it is ' flush ' and when it is sick."

The flush times are the years of unusual prosperity (like the period during the war), and in those years, they do an unusual amount of institutional advertising, not only in the magazines, newspapers and other mediums, but also in direct mail, without regard to results or expenditure — and then very abruptly there comes a sudden stop to most all their advertising.

The sick times are periods of depression, and then they cautiously but hastily turn to direct mail advertising for quick action results to help the salesmen get orders or to secure orders direct so that the wheels of the factory may be kept turning, and very often they expect the impossible from direct mail advertising.

These cycles " up and down " are unsound, expensive and generally bad for business and for advertising. The majority of advertisers create a lot of goodwill in prosperous times through institutional advertising, but fail to cash in on it when they need it most — because they do not have any consistent program of institutional building.

All of which clearly indicates that the average business executive does not enter into his problem of advertising and marketing on the basis of economics and fundamentals. He will set up reserves in his accounting and budgets for almost everything under the sun, including bad debts, machinery depreciation, inventory depreciation, real estate depreciation and dozens of other items, but not a cent for institutional promotion advertising and marketing in anticipation of an adverse period of selling — to be used in dull periods just as consistently as at other times.

But not so with Mr. Patterson. He seems to plan for adverse selling conditions, panics, and the like. He was a constant seeker of knowledge on advertising, merchandising and selling ideas, and the success of the National Cash Register Company (which started out under adverse conditions that would discourage almost anyone) typifies to a remarkable degree the value of mail advertising methods in building goodwill and prestige for an institution by mail.

My first acquaintance with Mr. Patterson dates back to an Associated Advertising Clubs Convention held in Philadelphia in 1916. There was a morning session devoted to a presentation of ideas from the various departments of advertising. William H. Ingersoll of the Ingersoll Watch Company was presiding and he had allotted 10 minutes to each speaker.

I was chosen to present direct mail advertising, and I found myself about tenth on the program. The first half dozen speakers exceeded their time to such an extent, that it resulted in Mr. Ingersoll limiting the remaining speakers to five minutes each.

When my turn came I was immediately attracted to a little man sitting in the very first row with a note book and pencil in his hand, intensely interested in the program and apparently making voluminous notes.

Under the pressure of having to make a ten-minute address in five minutes, I talked rapidly and with a degree of forcefulness and emphasis that brought forth an unusual amount of applause and appreciation from the little man in the front row. I wondered who he was and as I left the platform he followed me into the lobby and introduced himself. It was Mr. Patterson and he asked if I would let him have in writing an outline of my address.

I mention this experience merely to make clear that here was an executive at the head of a great business who was devoting a part of his time to a study of the advertising and selling side of his business by attendance at the advertising convention.

Yes, Mr. Patterson was an unusual personality, and personality is the greatest influence in business today. Many businesses have been built up around one or two individuals. Great businesses are very often the lengthened shadows of their founders.

Nevertheless, we àll know that the greatest successes in the business world are those which have endured long after the founders have passed into years of inactivity, and where house names have come to mean something more than the personality of an individual.

To build a business along permanent lines, we must get away from the fact that its success depends entirely on some one individual.

If a business is simply the projection of the personality of some outstanding figure, the moment that figure dies or passes into inactivity, the institution will suffer unless exceptional management saves it.

I take it that the objective of most people, in establishing a business, is to establish something for all time, not something which will die the moment the directing hand fails to function, but something which will continue and be a monument to their memory as well as a support to those they leave behind long after they have passed away.

For this reason it is advisable to use institutional merchandising methods which will establish the character of the house, rather than those which will merely draw attention to the personality of one individual, or of any individual connected with it in anything more than a subsidiary degree. In other words, the business should be primary and its individual executives should be secondary.

Just as it is possible to build up an individual's personality, so it is possible to build up the institutional prestige of a firm.

For developing and merchandising the characteristics in a business which make it recognized as a real success, mail advertising is of the greatest value. Carefully prepared, effectively produced advertising can impress on the public a high degree of appreciation of the firm's policies, inspire confidence and increase patronage.

Such houses as Marshall Field and Company, Carson, Pirie, Scott and Company, John Wanamaker, Tiffany's, Crane Company and Packard Motor Company have, through consistent institutional advertising, produced an impression of their personality and policies that has built an asset in prestige of incalculable value.

Sales Dependent on Individuality
have Hazardous Permanent Value

In most cases of selling to retailers, where the representation is through personal salesmen only, the sales are made on a personal basis. If a dealer gives his order to your representative because he likes him personally, the moment the salesman leaves your employ and goes to some other house it is not unlikely that he will carry the customer's trade with him.

This is true in a lesser degree in all matters of selling. Some clerks in retail stores are so well liked by customers that when they move to another store there is a certain following of customers who go with them.

While it is very desirable to employ salesmen who have the power to attract trade through their pleasing personality and manner of service, the main object of every proprietor of a business should at all times be to so develop the character of the institution that the institution itself will be the magnet that attracts the trade. If this is the case when a salesman ceases to be your representative and goes over to your rival's place of business, he will fail to carry the trade away from you.

Moreover, the salesman who may today be on especially good terms with your good customers may some day develop a fit of temper or some private grudge which will break off his personal friendship. In such a case, you stand a better chance of winning back the customer to your house if you have previously established a relationship of goodwill between the customer and your house.

The Unstable Position of the Wholesaler Who Pushes Another's Trademark Exclusively

A well-known automobile accessory house a few years ago devoted a large part of its catalog, and its sales efforts, to promoting a certain type of spark plug because of special arrangements which they had been able to make with the factory.

As a result of these sales efforts, the volume of sales of this particular spark plug were built up from practically nothing to a dominating place in the field.

Just at this time the manufacturers of the spark plug conceived the idea of selling to the trade direct and without warning to their previous wholesalers, changed their merchandising policy, eliminating the jobber altogether. Thus at one stroke, a very large volume of business was taken away from the wholesale house because its advertising and selling methods were devoted exclusively to pointing out the merits of the article sold, and had not devoted any time to selling the dealers on the merchant-service performed by themselves.

No matter how meritorious the article you are handling, a wholesaler's or retailer's own merchandising service — the thing which his business represents — should not be lost sight of in his merchandising plans.

Many people lose sight of the fact that a manufacturer can easily afford to spend money on advertising the particular article he produces and can establish a selling price to cover the cost of advertising. The wholesaler and retailer are in entirely different positions. The wholesale grocer, for instance, who would devote a lot of his time to advertising a certain brand of cereal, and so build up the major part of his trade on this particular article would lose the major part of his business if the manufacturer desired to eliminate the jobber and sell directly to the retailer.

In the marketing of products for consumer consumption it is necessary for the manufacturer to create consumer demand in order to gain the coöperation of dealers and jobbers. This is done through national advertising, direct mail advertising, and localized direct selling coöperation. This demand for the trade-marked article is an asset worth money to the manufacturer — frequently worth a fortune. One manufacturer of rubber canning rings has spent $300,000 in advertising during the past few years and estimates the goodwill established worth the profits of the business for the next ten years, or $3,000,000.

Where a wholesaler establishes between his home and the retailer a reputation for prompt service, for low prices, for courteous treatment, and for helpful suggestions and other similar acts of service, an asset will have been built up which no manufacturer can take away; and a condition will have been established so that if any manufacturer at any time desires to do his own merchandising he will be faced with the statement by the retailers, " We like to send all of our orders through So-

and-So.'' This next to the matter of capital required, is one of the best means of discouraging merchandising direct from the manufacturer that can be found.

The necessity for selling the institution by mail — or spreading broadcast the service rendered, and selling the quality and features of the merchandise, and its advantage to the buyer — devolves on the manufacturer primarily: the wholesaler will, but cannot afford to, do the necessary missionary work needed to popularize any one item. One of the common mistakes of the large manufacturer is the attempt to get away from the necessity for advertising.

The Insecurity of the Manufacturer Who Sells all of His Products to a Few Concerns

There are many concerns that make a practice of manufacturing goods for the definite order of large merchandisers. They rely on the volume of sales to these few houses to produce the profits.

When a manufacturer has a few good accounts of this kind which keep his factory working to capacity, he may imagine he is fixed for life. But, as a matter of fact, he is little better than an employe of a concern buying the article he makes, because at any time they can switch their orders to a rival manufacturer and the concern whose demand is good, but whose expenses are piling up, is left high and dry without any outlet for the finished products.

There are many instances of loss of big accounts in this way where manufacturers have borrowed and spent large sums of money to equip themselves to handle large orders only to find that these same orders were quickly removed and transferred to some rival or manufactured by the buying concern independently at a cost they consider to their advantage. There are so many manufacturers following this dangerous policy of treading on thin ice that I want to take this occasion to caution all manufacturers as to the necessity of creating a solid foundation for their demand through advertising, and establishing in the minds of thousands of people the merits of the goods produced.

Whether or not the manufacturer who produces merchandise has anything to do with the merchandising of the article produced, it is wise policy for him to keep in touch with those who use it, and sell it in a retail way, and if stenciled products are sold in quantities, a sufficient line should be produced and sold under the firm's trade name to assure the manufacturer independence if his customers should cease buying.

It is good psychology to put the picture of the factory on the advertising of a washing machine. The woman who buys the machine knows that back of it is a big factory, reassuring her that she should always be able to secure any parts which might need replacing.

If by means of mail merchandising methods the various dealers handling a particular product can be induced to use advertising showing that the article is produced in a modern, well equipped, daylight factory, a permanent hold on the trade will possibly be established because the organization has been made a part of the reason for the purchase.

When the German manufacturers flooded our markets with cheap German safety razors, selling as low as 25 cents, had it not been for the cumulative effect of years of institutional advertising, the Gillette Company would have suffered greatly. For the same reason the Westclox products hold their own in competition with cheap foreign alarm clocks, because they have consistently advertised year after year. Had they advertised in a spasmodic way when sales were slow the inroads of foreign competition would be seriously felt.

If the wholesaler and the retailer are allowed to talk solely of their service, and nothing is said regarding the manufacturer's part in the production of the goods, the buyer then sees the service as the supreme thing, and the goods as only secondary.

We have demonstrated where the wholesaler who did the manufacturers' advertising for him was placed in a false position, and we have shown where the manufacturer who relied on the wholesaler to do his advertising for him was also placed in an insecure position; and if both wholesaler and manufacturer assume that the retailer will be willing or able to create local demand for them, they must be sorely disappointed because the function of the retailer is to advertise his own store, and his own service to the people whom he is supposed to serve, and this part of the service he must surely do or his business will suffer.

The third phase of this question of appropriate advertising is covered by the man who does the actual retailing, and here we find the same mistake as we find in the case of the wholesaler and the manufacturer. He very frequently relies on the other fellow to do his advertising and when he does, he is stepping on dangerous ground.

An actual case will probably make this clearer. A representative for a washing machine concern spent twelve years of his life talking up the merits of the machine, ironer, and vacuum cleaner, and he relied on the company to supply him with all of the advertising. Everything that went out from his agency went out on the letterhead and under the signature of the manufacturer he was representing.

This man had built up a splendid business, appointing sub-agents and establishing branch stores. At the end of ten years, the washing machine company decided to do its own selling, and all of the advertising and business building that this particular agent had done was immediately nullified because he had failed to talk about his service and had failed to sell people on the accommodations that he had given. Consequently, when he found it advisable to push another make of machine, he found that fully 50 per cent of his business stayed with the old company because the advertising was done under the identity of the manufacturer.

On the other hand there is the case of a representative, who so successfully advertised his service, and talked so much about the value of the free repair features and other services that he gave, about the splendid accommodations he extended, and about so many things that were peculiarly his own, that when the company whom he was representing decided that it would be well to investigate the matter of doing their own selling, they found him so firmly entrenched in the field that they abandoned the idea at once.

The lesson is obvious. Merchandising by mail should tell your story to your customers in such a way as to bind them to you, and if I have repeated this statement to you several times in this chapter, it is because I want to impress on the minds of readers that this is one of the fundamentals of advertising, and that direct mail pieces are not profitable alone in proportion to the number and regularity of the pieces mailed out, but their success is vitally dependent on the identity which the sales appeals are built around.

The Dependability of the Volume of Business Produced by Selling The Institution by Mail

One of the big problems of every sales manager is to find a basis of selling that can be relied upon.

For instance, you send out a salesman in certain territory in Iowa. He goes out and without any particular help produces $250,000 worth of business in a year. This should not be taken as a basis, for you will find that the man you assigned to the Ohio territory will sell a very different volume from the man who travels in Illinois, and that the variation in the selling ability of any individual is something that cannot be computed ahead of time; at the same time the sales resistance, conditions in territory, competition and so on, influence sales.

I know of salesmen in the same organization,

traveling practically the same territory, whose returns in volume of orders vary from twenty thousand dollars a year to two hundred thousand dollars a year, and the answer is, the personality of the man and his sales efficiency.

The same thing is true of selling through agents. One agent will comb a territory completely, produce a large volume of orders, and establish a good name for your concern and your product. Another agent will produce a small volume of orders, and get you " in bad " with customers.

Selling through the dealer produces similar results. Whereas one dealer will be the leading light in his town and your goods will gain prestige by being identified with his store, another dealer will not have such an excellent presentation and your goods will suffer from the very fact that he is permitted to handle them.

The volume of orders received from dealers varies greatly. The " live wire " sells a satisfactory volume, but those who are not used to modern merchandising will produce but indifferent results, and the great majority of dealers are those whose sales efforts are mediocre and who need specific education and help from the manufacturers to succeed in a real way.

Mail promotional methods place the manufacturer in a position to exert a splendid influence on his dealers and place them in position to sell a larger volume of goods. The presentation in merchandising by mail is always uniform and as effective as the experience and talent of capable mail merchandisers can make it. The imperfections of individual salesmen do not enter into the mail presentation. Your story is told as well as it is possible for the most skilled illustrators and the best copy writers to tell it. You have time to review it before it is sent out, and it is a pretty safe shot that where 10,000 mailing pieces bring in a certain volume of replies, in the state of Iowa, 10,000 mailing pieces mailed in the state of Illinois will do practically the same thing. This gives to the sales manager a stability of results and an assurance of steady inquiries which he is unable to obtain by any other means.

It enables the manufacturer to feature his line regularly before the trade, keep his house, merchandise and service before the dealer, induce the dealer to use his helps and drive for bigger business in this line. He is able frequently to reach the dealers' clerks and instruct them in salesmanship talking points.

He can couple up the triangle by operating a mail campaign to jobbers and their salesmen, at the same time benefiting himself, building goodwill and helping each coöperating channel to move more goods and make better profits.

CHAPTER IX

FINANCING A MAIL SELLING CAMPAIGN

OF all methods of advertising and merchandising, marketing by mail is the easiest to finance and control. You do not have to risk a small fortune in a blind plunge when this method is followed. Any proposition which will not show results on a $500 or $1,000 test campaign will usually fail in the same way, no matter how much money you put into it. Feel your way very carefully. Drop any proposition just as soon as you have had time to give it a fair trial and do not get the necessary average of returns. If the average comes up to normal on a test campaign, then you can safely back that same plan in an unlimited way, and to your ever-increasing profit.

The law of averages works out in a never-failing way in selling by mail. If you have a carefully prepared selling plan, which may combine letters, folders, or other mailing pieces that will produce a certain amount of

inquiries or orders direct on an initial investment of $500, the same proportionate quantity
will, in nearly every case, come in as the result
of a $5000 or $10,000 investment. As your
advertising investment increases, your net
profit margin will invariably increase in equal
proportion for the reason that as your business
grows you reduce overhead and operating
costs by buying larger units of advertising
and printed matter at lower costs.

I do not mean by this that the smaller campaign will put the proposition immediately
on a self-supporting basis. It is not often
that such a thing is possible, particularly on a
new business starting at scratch. But it will
show you the lay of the land, and will guide
you in determining what you can expect to
pay on an average for your inquiries, how
many follow-ups will be necessary to get the
maximum results from your expenditures and
what percentage of sales you can reasonably
depend on securing.

The important qualifying statement I give
you in this connection is first, last and all the
time, your success will depend on carefully
prepared plans, well-written copy and properly printed follow-up literature; a selection of

the very best lists and a proper analysis of your market.

If your initial venture does not show a profit, or at least indicate that a profit can be secured, with a sufficient volume of business to offset operating expenses, then you should try other tests or discard the proposition entirely.

As your experience broadens as a result of these tests, you will be better able to discriminate between the impossible and the practical in the development of a permanent and successful business in mail selling.

You may have the good fortune to develop a winner on your first tryout, and if you do you should lose no time in going after the necessary volume of business in order to begin banking the profits before your working capital has been exhausted.

Mr. John C. Sweeney, Advising Director of the International Correspondence Schools, one of the best known authorities on present-day marketing, once said: " There isn't any method of marketing that enables one to mark his progress every inch of the way so well and so unmistakably as selling by mail."

With any other plan of selling; through

national advertising; through the employment of a corps of specialty salesmen, or through the selection of a store location in the heart of a business district, the business man is committed to a large expenditure without knowing definitely what his returns will be, but in marketing by mail, he can make tests, and determine by small expenditures what to expect from any given appropriation.

This problem is presented in a very distinctive way by Mr. Sweeney: " For one hundred dollars, or two hundred dollars, we can test out our plan on 1000 people, and the reaction we get from this 1000 will be a good indication of what we can expect on a larger scale."

How important this is, is indicated by his further statement: " When you fall down, it is much easier to look your management square in the face and charge $100 to experience and get by with it." How large a factor this is in effecting economy, is also indicated by the fact that the International Correspondence Schools, and their related institution, the Woman's Institute, spends over $300,000 in a single year in postage stamps alone.

In the case of a large corporation where the volume of sales reaches large figures, a definite appropriation, amounting to at least 25 per cent of the total advertising budget, should be set aside for mail selling and promotion. If the test method is decided on, the small list can first be used, and the final appropriation can then be used on the most successful advertising pieces as determined by the test.

There are, of course, some regular routine expenditures in the mail selling field where tests are neither necessary nor possible, because the purpose of the pieces being mailed out is to create goodwill and not to produce orders or leads. I refer to such mailing pieces as house organs. A definite appropriation to take care of these publications will be entirely separate from any of the mail selling budgets.

Even in the case of house organs it is possible to start in with a small appropriation and reach intensively a small section of the field, and gradually build up. Say, for instance, that in your total sales territory, you have 200,000 prospects — dealers who handle your line. It is possible to limit your intensive efforts to a state or a county, and from an initial issue of 2000 gradually increase your appropriation for the house magazine until you are covering the complete field. In this way you can determine the value of the house organ as a goodwill builder.

In the case of a young company just starting up, it would be almost suicidal to attempt to cover the entire field with a direct mail campaign which consumed a large part of their funds. It would be far better for them to make tests — even paying the premium of high cost for small volume — and establish proof of the pulling power of certain types of advertising before making any particular plunge.

An instance of inexpensive financing is demonstrated by the following test, made through mail methods to find a market for a side-line product:

One of the big Chicago packing concerns handled a full line of musical instruments and gut strings, and sold the line through salesmen.

The instruments were discontinued and the strings were not enough of an item to make a profitable line for salesmen.

A carefully prepared combination illustrated house organ-circular-price list was sent to a selected list of 10,000 music dealers.

The first mailing brought not hundreds —

but *thousands* of orders. It is the more remarkable as this was done during July and August, when the season for these products is notoriously poor.

The sale of gut strings by this company is now left entirely to the little monthly messenger. The former salesmen have been assigned to other lines.

It is astonishing how many people entertain private ambitions to get into the mail order field. Very frequently men who are successful in their particular business, executives of large corporations, presidents of banks, lawyers and insurance men come to our offices with some sort of a device or specialty in which they have become interested and they want to market the proposition by mail.

When it is explained to them by simple facts and figures that the cost of reaching the market and of placing the article in the hands of the ultimate consumer takes away all of the profit in the article itself, they are surprised at this, and wonder how it is possible for mail order houses to finance their campaigns.

The secret of the whole matter lies in that old established principle of merchandising, that the profit of any article in the mail order field comes from repeat orders. In financing any selling campaign, it requires a knowledge of merchandising fundamentals, and any person who wants to enter the mail order field should first of all make sure that he has an article which has repeat possibilities, or one that has a wide spread between cost of producing and selling price.

The statements frequently made about the inexpensive character of direct mail advertising and the profitable nature of returns, have prompted many people to reason: " Why, sure, we can't lose — let's just inaugurate a mail advertising campaign, and the returns will pay for all the expenses and give us a nice profit." Such reasoning is fallacious and should be discouraged. Remember that marketing by mail is a science which demands as close attention to preparation and plans as any other phase of the field of merchandising.

Just as it is necessary to plan ahead and appropriate a sufficient amount of capital to satisfy your landlord for rental of the location, and just as it is necessary to place a large amount of capital in fixtures which will bring you no immediate returns, and just as it is necessary to arrange for capital to provide your stock, and to provide for the salaries of employes and other expenses incident to up-keep, so it is necessary to provide capital for merchandising by mail.

Appropriating a Portion of Selling Cost to Pay for Mail Selling

As has been shown in previous chapters, marketing by mail is only one of many successful methods of merchandising, and it is most successful where it is correlated with other methods of selling. The functions of marketing by mail are clearly defined. They vary with different types of products, and with different types of customers.

Sometimes a much larger proportion of national advertising should be used than direct mail advertising. In other cases, the direct mail selling should bear the main brunt of publicity. Sometimes the direct mail campaign merely does missionary work, and all of the sales are made by personal " closers." Sometimes direct mail methods are used to close the inquiries which national advertising has produced. Whichever method is selected after a thorough analysis of the selling conditions, suitable appropriations should be made to cover the cost of the advertising requirements. It is a wise policy to adopt a " budget " plan which provides at the beginning of each financial year a definite schedule of expenditures in each department.

Let us say, for instance, that a conference of business executives, acting on the advice of expert counsel in each department, has decided that the most economic basis of selling will be to use fifty per cent of their selling cost for salesmen, twenty-five per cent for national advertising and twenty-five per cent for direct mail. If this twenty-five per cent to be spent for direct advertising represents the sum of, say, $12,000, it is then put up to the advertising manager to decide how this $12,000 shall be laid out during the year to produce maximum results; but there should, in every case, be an appropriation of this kind made. This is true in all types of business, whether it is selling oil stock, food products, machinery, clothing or services.

How an Advertising Budget is Made up to Include Mail Selling

The methods of business executives in making up a budget are many and varied. Sometimes the chief executive himself decides in an arbitrary way: " We will cut out the trade paper advertising this year, and put it into direct mail." Or he may say: " Let's reduce our national advertising appropriation about $10,000 this year and apply it to direct mail work."

The chief executive may call in his agency, advertising manager and sales manager, and may rely on their judgments as to the appropriation for advertising, both in the national field and in the direct mail work. In this case, there may be personal prejudices behind the views.

In other cases, the executive calls into conference the interested department heads and experts in the particular field, and after having a statement of the prospects of sales from the sales manager, the capacity for production from the factory manager, the financial standing from the accountant, and the recommendations of the advertising manager or the counsel on national advertising and direct mail work, he arrives at a decision where it is possible for all departments to coöperate.

The classification of these department heads, of course, varies in different institutions. For instance, in a wholesale house, the buyer would be substituted for the production manager. In a retail store, the recommendations would not be on national advertising, but on local advertising through newspapers and the other available channels.

In some houses no definite budget is made. The different department heads make recommendations from time to time, and endeavor to get through appropriations for some particular needs.

It is always a wise policy to lay aside a fund for emergency publicity purposes. It is frequently desirable to put out a special mailing, an announcement to the trade or make a special drive for sales in some dealer's locality. Whatever method is used, whether it is left to the decision of one individual, to two or three in conference, to a group meeting of all interested executives, or any other means of appropriating the funds, the chief executive should keep his hands on the reins and decide with clear judgment that no worth-while selling medium should be neglected, and that no phase of his business should receive too much attention to the detriment of other departments.

When the chief executive realizes the profitable nature and many possibilities for influencing the field by mail, and contemplates correlating it with other selling agencies in building up his sales volume, there will be no question about his decision to set aside a goodly appropriation for direct mail advertising.

In determining the advertising appropriation, one experienced executive believes it is well to be guided not so much by an arbitrary fixed sum as by the results you want to get, and when the desired results are decided on to set aside an advertising investment necessary to accomplish the objective.

Definite Appropriations Should be Decided on

A definite percentage of advertising should be figured in both good times and bad. The plan of spending money for advertising to stimulate inquiries and sales only in times when sales fall off is inefficient. The safest plan is to have a definite policy backed by a tentative appropriation budgeted for the entire year. That is the policy followed by the Johnson Educator Cracker Company, Cambridge, Massachusetts. The president of that company recently said: " We look upon advertising as just as necessary an item of expense as packages, production, delivery expense, and so on. We make it a rule at our company to figure on a five per cent advertising allowance in all list prices. Hence, we are in a position to know what we can do in an advertising way at all times and do not overspend or underspend."

The appropriation set aside for advertising will always vary in confirmation with business conditions, competition and other influences. It is largely influenced also by the margin of profit and by the plan of selling.

The following percentages of total earnings spent annually for advertising, under normal selling conditions, may be a guide to many advertisers in deciding on the percentage of gross sales that should be applied to advertising:

Campbell's Soups .... 2.4 per cent
Furniture Manufacturers ...... 2.4 " "
Grape Juice .... 10 " "
Mail Order Houses .... 10 " "
Tobacco Manufacturers .... 5 " "
Cigarette Manufacturers .... 6 " "
Phonograph Manufacturers .... 5 " "
Paint Manufacturers .... $3\frac{1}{2}$ " "
Men's Collars .... $3\frac{1}{2}$ " "
Kodak Manufacturers .... 3 " "
Soap (Ivory) Manufacturers ... 3 " "
Old Dutch Cleanser .... 10 " "
Toilet Preparations .... $2\frac{1}{2}$ " "
Men's Clothing .... 2 " "
Printers .... $2\frac{1}{2}$ " "
Stove Manufacturers .... $2\frac{1}{5}$ " "
Auto Manufacturers .... $\frac{1}{8}$ " "
Washing Machines .... 3.2 " "
Wrigley's Gum .... 14 " "

Some lines, such as railroads, spent far less than warranted for advertising until quite recently when the need for advertising became apparent to railroad executives. Timely attention is more generally being given to systematic advertising in a more aggressive way.

The basis for determining how much this appropriation should be was given in Chapter II, which dealt specifically with statistics.

*Proportion of Mail and National Advertising
Used by Large Merchandisers.*

A question frequently asked is one regarding the proportion of direct mail advertising used by large merchandisers as compared to general publicity. This varies with the nature of the business, the type of the institution, and the policy of the house.

It goes without saying, for instance, that Sears, Roebuck and Company expends a much larger percentage of its advertising appropriation for direct mail work than a neighborhood store. It is also true that the neighborhood store which depends so largely on the personal visits of the inhabitants within a radius of a few blocks, is a neighborhood store largely because it has decided to be one and has not used any of the long range methods of advertising.

Stores in the larger centers are awakening to the fact that they can increase their volume of business materially by the use of direct mail, and the retail store of Marshall Field and Company now uses twenty-five per cent of its advertising appropriation for direct mail advertising as against seventy-five per cent for newspaper and other forms of publicity. Fifteen years ago ninety per cent was spent for newspapers and ten per cent for direct mail promotion. This is typical of the trend of advertising appropriations in the retail field.

The most successful retailers in the country are advertising more and more by mail. Fred Mann in his very successful retail store at Devils Lake, North Dakota, advertises all over his section by mail. So do Garver Brothers who operate a general store in Strassburg, Ohio, where a weak local newspaper medium makes direct mail methods imperative.

Even the smaller retail store which has confined its advertising efforts largely to local newspaper advertising finds, when it adopts a consistent policy of merchandising by mail, that the volume of business is materially increased, and that they are able to sell the people who previously were considered outside their radius.

It is my recommendation to the average retail store in this country, that it spend a dollar in direct mail advertising for every dollar spent in newspapers. If this plan is followed with a consistent program of merchandising, business can be increased to almost unbelievable proportions.

With the excellent delivery system of present day motor trucks, the range of service of the average store has been materially increased, and to take advantage of this increased range of business it is necessary to use longer range methods of selling.

Accordingly a great mail order wholesale house has found it expedient to syndicate a monthly newspaper to dealers, with their headings, their names, their advertisements and so on, with fifty per cent of editorial matter of interest to women. Results have been exceptional. The paper has grown in size and features and about ninety per cent of the expiring service is renewed each year.

Similarly, the wholesale house, which has been limited because of the high cost of personal salesmen, who have confined their sales effort to the territory where personal sales methods can be profitably used, can extend this area by applying direct mail methods. Consequently the appropriations of wholesale houses for direct mail campaigns to supplement the effort of their salesmen are gradually on the increase. Direct mail advertising is reducing the sales cost and adding a larger volume of business at proportionately lower expense.

The manufacturer who previously confined his advertising efforts to general publicity with the object of creating consumer demand, finds that the educational influence of general publicity is not enough to secure the order, but that it is necessary to link up selling connections through wholesalers and retailers in order to secure the order. The increasing volume of direct mail pieces furnished by the manufacturer to the wholesaler, and also to the retailer, shows the trend of merchandising thought toward direct presentation of the merits of the article to the person who actually buys it in conjunction with a recognition of the sales agency through which the article may be purchased.

In an investigation made among seventy-four large manufacturers who did national advertising, it was found that the average percentage spent for direct mail was about twenty-five per cent. It seems that this percentage is a fair average today. It must be borne in mind that there is an increase of one or more per cent in this division annually, and in computing this percentage, window trims, display cards and other dealer helps are not included, although literature for store distribution is included.

While no definite percentage can be given which would apply to all cases regarding the amount of direct mail advertising, and national publicity, it is safe to say that one should keep pace with the other and there should be consistent relationship between the two. By that I mean that when the personal sales organization for distribution of closing orders is limited to restricted territory, then national advertising covering the whole country would be largely wasteful. To get the utmost good from advertising it should be supported by a complete selling plan embracing the whole territory covered by the mediums used. Advertisers should bear in mind that the complete sale is made by having the public educated to desire a certain article, and the merchant educated not only to stock the article, but to display and sell it.

So, in financing a selling campaign, provision should be made, not merely for general publicity and representation, but for actual selling direct from the dealer to the consumer.

CHAPTER X

REGULATING THE MARKET BY MAIL

When stagnant selling conditions hit a business, nine out of ten executives or heads of businesses run to cover, and begin a program of curtailment in their sales and advertising that is painfully tragic.

In these periods, however, it is observed that there are some experienced merchandisers who bring into play, with greater stimulus, mail selling methods, and who, as a result of this wise policy, maintain a satisfactory sales volume while their timid and panicky competitors are hitting the toboggan.

It is in these trying and difficult periods of marketing that mail selling can be used to the best possible advantage in regulating your market, and here are the reasons:

1 You can get quick action in reaching any given territory. You can take advantage of buying conditions that are favorable in any trade territory,

197

and omit from your intensive sales follow-up work territories that are poor for business.

2 Your sales strategy is hidden from your competitors. You don't have to show your hand.

3 You can appeal to all or any group of your customers or prospects by dividing your lists into proper units. You can talk straight to each unit in terms of merchandise, price and service that is directly applicable to their business.

4 You can accurately key your results and know just how each sales effort is paying out.

5 You can place in the hands of each prospect and customer not only your merchandise offers, but you can give them at the same time an order blank, a reply card or return envelope or other means for a prompt and convenient method of reply.

No other form of marketing and advertising offers these same advantages.

I want to particularly emphasize the " quick action " feature of marketing by mail, because this method, and this one alone, offers the opportunity for you to reach practically overnight by first-class mail, 5,000 or 10,000 or more of your prospects and customers, in all parts of the country, or in any given territory, as a study of market conditions may determine.

I have chosen to call direct mail selling the "pinch hit" method of advertising. When the order file is getting very low in the factory, and there is a prospect of idle machinery and layoffs, a "pinch hitter" is needed, but the head of nearly any manufacturing plant gets cold feet on advertising for the next month or the few months ahead. He needs orders today, tomorrow and the next day. How can he get them? By direct mail advertising — marketing by mail — an aggressive plan of going after business intensively.

Don't let "market conditions" get the best of you.

No one knows better than a man actually directing a business how quickly an unusual situation can cause people to stop buying. The seasons affect every business either favorably or unfavorably. A coal strike in the anthracite field, a crop failure in another territory or conditions in the textile industry may cause a period of idleness.

Mail advertising can be quickly adjusted to meet these sudden developments in buying conditions. It is under your control right up to the minute you put it into the mails. There are no advance schedules where you O.K. copy three to six weeks ahead of the appearance of your advertising and sales story.

You can apply mail advertising methods to regulate buying conditions and to keep the sales curve in your business more balanced and not so subject to violent fluctuation, due to unfavorable business conditions.

The successful business man is the one who so operates that he can set aside a reserve from his profits and keep his mail advertising going in season and out of season. When business is good he always has enough funds to keep his advertising in action. When business tends to slacken, he then draws on his reserve to keep his mail advertising going, because this is the time he needs it the most.

Value and Sources of Market Information

Every business man who aims to keep abreast of the times has ready access to some sort of statistical information governing the trend of business.

The many authoritative sources of information on this subject, such as that conducted by the Babson Statistical Bureau, the Harvard Research Bureau, Standard Statistics Company and other similar organizations, furnish information to the business man which shows him the reasons for the fluctuations in business as well as prophesying conditions in the future. They not only measure the tide of prosperity, but show why conditions are good. Where an unnatural condition exists, they point to the logical trend of such unnatural condition. They aid in gauging business conditions that lie ahead of the different communities.

According to one of the statistical companies, the measure of business prosperity is the measure of business activity. Men make money when business is active. They have little money to spend when business slows down. The purchasing power of any community depends not solely on population or wealth per capita. It depends also on relative business prosperity. Obviously a manufacturer considering a mail order campaign would find it to his advantage to concentrate his efforts on the parts of the country where the people have been stimulated in buying activity.

Leading economists have long given thought to the regulation of the tide of business with the object of preventing panics on one hand and arresting booms on the other. The Federal Reserve Act was a result of the application of the economists' minds in statecraft to the business problems of the country along this line.

Experienced business executives know that the main hazards in business are incurred during these periods of inflation and deflation, and they know that if in their own case they can eliminate the risk brought about by these high points and low points in business, they will have greater assurance of a continuation of a more uniformly profitable business.

As has been pointed out by many of the statistical research bureaus, marketing by mail is a very potential factor in meeting these changing business conditions, and the statistical bureaus have repeatedly urged the use of the mails to counteract the falling off of business at a time of sudden depression, and also to counteract any false prosperity which may occur in boom times.

Counteracting Business Slumps

If there is ever a time when quick selling methods are needed, it is when prices begin to fall. To unload quickly when prices begin to tumble is the objective of every sales manager.

Those who study the market, and who will take the time to analyze statistics, have little difficulty in anticipating a shortage of orders. Statistics are now so far developed that the amount of stock on hand of any given line can be accurately gauged. When stocks in the hands of the dealers reach a certain high point, and consumer demand threatens to fall off, a reduction in orders from dealers must logically be anticipated.

The sales manager of a modern business, confronted with such a problem, finds himself in need of " quick action " methods, for he must reach thousands of dealers located, many of them, hundreds of miles away and make arrangements to dispose of his stock so that his firm will not be caught with a big surplus when prices tumble and find it necessary to make disastrous reductions in their inventory as a consequence.

Business policy will, of course, dictate the wise course to pursue. It may be that the management will decide to take a five per cent loss on present stock on hand rather than to hold it and possibly sustain a twenty per cent loss. If this is the policy decided on, an announcement of these reduced prices sent out by mail will reach the dealers, and dispose of the stocks on hand before competitors have had an opportunity to follow a similar policy.

To make sure of the complete success of a plan of this kind, all of the salesmen out on the road should also be reached by mail and advised of the company's policy, so that the sales personally made will have the added impetus of the lower price and give the house an increased volume of sales from this direction.

As a matter of fact, the salesmen should

receive a monthly bulletin through which they can be kept in close touch with conditions, prices, and so on, as well as with the information which they should be given. It has also been deemed good policy in a number of instances to take all of the dealers into the confidence of the manufacturer or wholesaler, carrying out this policy, and to advise them by mail that, " Now is the time to dispose of these articles on hand at special bargain prices because they can be replaced at lower cost."

By carrying this sales method through to the ultimate consumer, you have given the consumer, who was hesitating about making any further purchases, an incentive to keep on buying, and have in this way delayed the business slump right at the source and helped to regulate market conditions.

Preparing Campaigns to Overcome Depression

Students of psychology tell us that business depressions are largely mental. We know that this is true, and while financial resources and the material facts of over or under production enter into the law of supply and demand, certain and disastrous drops in the market, and the seasons of frenzied buying, do result from the mental attitude of the buyer.

So far it has not been possible to get any statistics which show the number of people who were induced to buy, and the result of the propaganda carried on during the period of reconstruction after the late World War, but it is a fact, that the propaganda of optimism carried on through the newspapers, by personal talks to business executives, but still more largely if not quite so obviously, through the medium of direct mail, was the thing that restored the buying spirit of the American public, and saved the nation from a much worse period of depression than might otherwise have fallen upon us.

The healthy and vigorous sales effort at a time when business was low was the thing that saved the day.

The business house which applies itself to the task of regulating business so as to avoid, on the one hand, a period of idleness, small orders, poor collections and inflated overhead, and, on the other hand, a deluge of orders with consequent shortages of material, high priced help, financial strain, and dissatisfied customers will find it easily possible to keep in touch with its selling agents throughout the country and advise them regarding the trend of business conditions in their particular field.

There is a tendency in this direction already. The number of firms who issue bulletins containing a business review is increasing, and the number of other firms who include in their various house bulletins, trade magazines, and other mailing pieces, information on the trend of market conditions, shows that they recognize the value of regulating the market. There are about 2000 house publications published in this country today and a considerable percentage are used, in part, for trade educational purposes.

The individual manufacturer or wholesaler, can, if his business is a large enough one, well afford to distribute this information himself, but there are many instances where associations of business men get together and promote this type of information for the good of the trade generally.

Most people recognize the value of vigorous, persistent, and unyielding optimism suggested through the mails. It is interesting to note that the fluctuations in business recorded by various firms seem to show a corresponding ratio between the healthy nature of their direct mail propaganda during business depression, and the volume of business they were able to maintain throughout this period.

An instance which demonstrates this case very clearly is that of two concerns, each making pipe fittings. One, when the period of depression came, started on the policy: " Whatever isn't actually producing, we must eliminate." The first thing to fall beneath the pruning knife was the house organ, a newsy little messenger of goodwill which they had been sending out to buyers of their products. By discontinuing this publication for a year they saved about $4000.00.

The other house, manufacturing a similar line, regarded their house organ as their one means of combating the tendency of the buyer to hold off placing orders. They gave increased attention to the publication of their magazine, enlarged it, put in new illustrations, and in general incurred an expenditure of an additional $2000.00. The more the buyers showed a tendency to discontinue their purchases, the more vigorously the little house organ fought — it was pulling up-stream against the tide.

At the end of the year of depression, the house which had discontinued their house publication showed a loss in business of $48,000 and a loss of seventy-three customers on the books.

For the same period, the house which had continued the fight for business by the little house organ sent through the mail, showed a loss of only $5,000.00 in total volume of business, and an increase in number of customers on their books of seventeen.

But these figures do not tell such a significant story as the ones which appeared in the following year.

The firm which had sustained a large loss in business, and had discontinued one of its best selling efforts, found itself under the necessity of fighting an uphill game, while the house which had continued its mail selling efforts strenuously found itself already a long way up the grade. The increase of business for the following year (one of moderate prosperity) showed the following figures:

For the house which had discontinued the house magazine for a year and started only when business conditions were good again, there was a recorded increase of $18,000 in business, and of fourteen new customers.

The firm which had been consistently advertising showed an increase in business of $73,000 and the addition of thirty-two new names on their ledgers.

These many evidences of the value of mail merchandising methods in overcoming depression, show that there are tremendous possibilities ahead of the business men of America as soon as they all recognize the fact that the time when business is poor is the time to fight most strenuously for its restoration.

Broadcasting Price Changes Without Competitors' Knowledge

In all lines of industry, prices affect the volume of trade. In fact with most of us, the things we buy depend largely on the price. If it were not for the difference in price, more men would drive a Rolls-Royce, and fewer would drive Fords. The determining factor of whether I buy a Dodge or a Buick or a

Packard is the price — it is how much I can afford.

Values are fine things to talk about, but if you have a suit that costs $100, and the workman has only $25 to spend for a suit, all of the advertising in the world and all the salesmanship ever devised couldn't sell the hundred dollar suit to the workman who only had $25.

The law of supply and demand is regulated largely by the matter of price and because of this fact, it becomes necessary for the sales manager to get any revision of prices quickly before the people who buy his product, in order to bring in the known increase in orders as a result of the lower prices.

There are various ways of doing this. We have all seen the advertisements of the automobile companies who announce in large type in the leading newspapers and national magazines, a reduction in the price on their cars. Such a public announcement gets immediately to the attention of competitive manufacturers, and enables them to make immediate moves to counter any advantage you may have gained.

Word sent out through personal salesmen takes a long time to reach the buyer, because very frequently the salesman is several weeks on his trip.

If while the salesman is out, your competitor sends out a notice through the mails announcing a lower price, you will find that your personal salesman will come on back to the office with a very meager budget of orders. The competitor who took advantage of the quicker method of announcing his price through the mail will have received the orders before your salesmen will have had a chance to present his case, and, most likely, you will know nothing about what your competitor has been doing.

The point we want to emphasize at this time has nothing to do with that long intermittent period known as depression, but with the regular marketing which is conducted so extensively by means of the price list sent out at regular intervals, and here, again, we want to emphasize the value of speed.

Some time ago, we were called in by an organization who reported a loss of sales, which they could not understand. They had been doing business largely by sending out bulletins and price lists the first of every month. These price lists would be printed ahead of time and completed about the 20th, and the organization felt that they were saving money by having the girls in the office insert these price lists in envelopes during their spare time in the ten intervening days.

Sometimes the girls would have enough spare time to complete the mailing by the first of the month. Sometimes the mailing would drag on until the 4th, 5th and 6th. An analysis of the field showed that their competitors would revise their prices right down to the 28th of the month, and that mailings would be all completed on the 31st so as to reach their customers on the first of the month.

A comparison of prices showed that in between the 20th and 28th, very frequently price changes occurred which made a great difference in the buyer's preference, so that he would be confronted with the comparison of prices showing 25 cents in one list, and 28 cents in the other. When this was continued over a long period of months, the buyer came to regard the one house, which had been slow in its methods, as a high-priced house as compared with competitors. As a matter of fact, the prices were actually identical but the slowness of issuing the price list made the apparent difference.

As soon as conditions were changed, and the price lists were issued in a business-like way by a house equipped to handle the mailing in a few hours' time, this organization began to pick up and, in a little while, it was restored to its previous position of dominating the field.

This clearly shows that the competitor, by sending his price lists out quietly and reaching a field of hundreds of miles without letting his rival know, had been the means of taking away a large part of the business, and it demonstrates the need for quick action where price changes are concerned.

Maintaining Prices by Sending out Goodwill Messengers

As pointed out in one of the earlier chapters, it is a dangerous policy for any firm to be guided only by market conditions, or by competitors' prices in determining the prices which they will charge for their goods.

When factory costs show that it is necessary to maintain certain prices, and you find that your competitors are selling below this price, it would be a foolish policy to reduce your prices and in this way conduct your business at a loss. It is only a matter of time when prices which do not permit of profit eliminate themselves, because the firm selling at these prices is headed for bankruptcy.

One of the common occurrences in the field of business is for some organization to start selling goods at impossible prices, and there is hardly any field of industry which is free from this menace of the unfair price cutter. It has been repeatedly demonstrated, however, that prices can be maintained by reputable houses in spite of competition of this kind.

A few years ago we witnessed a price cutting onslaught in the tire manufacturing field. Tires were offered at prices about half what was charged by the makers of standard automobile tires. For these manufacturers to sit idly by would have been poor policy, and to have cut their prices in an effort to meet unfair competition would have been equally foolish.

Thanks to a well organized mail selling plan, all dealers selling such lines as the Goodyear, Goodrich and other standard lines were kept advised as to the right sales policy, and the value of the reputation of the large manufacturers, the worth of his guarantee as compared to the guarantee of some unknown concern, and many other points of sound economic policy were repeatedly sent to the dealers, showing them how they could continue to sell standard makes of tires at regular prices, far above that asked by competitors.

Price cutting dealers are likely to become panicky, because of the apparent sales advantage of their low-priced competitors. Messages of encouragement and helpfulness are eagerly looked forward to, and the mail campaign which carries these messages will make dealers better merchandisers.

Showing the real advantage of being associated with a quality product is a very potent factor in maintaining the volume of sales. Hart, Shaffner & Marx, by distributing 3,000,000 style books through their dealers twice a year, spring and fall, maintain a quality reputation which not only stimulates the demand for the clothes they manufacture, but makes their dealers loyal and satisfied that they are pursuing correct merchandising policies by linking their sales efforts with an article of known merchandising value, and the mail selling efforts of Hart, Schaffner & Marx have proved a complete antidote for the clothing dealer opposition which advertises the propaganda, " Save $10.00 on Your Suits."

Whenever an epidemic of "low-priced" competition shows itself, you will find that the mails offer you a splendid means of regulating the market, for steadying trade and restoring the confidence of the dealers associated with you in marketing your product.

For emergencies of this kind you will find the access to the dealer a great deal easier when you have already established the lines of communication in the shape of regular, direct-mailing pieces, giving the dealer counsel on his merchandising problem. In fact, it will be found one of the best methods of regulating the market at all times to keep the dealer on your mailing list, and keep him supplied with the necessary information to make him an intelligent coöperator in merchandising your articles.

Then when an emergency arises the advice that you give him will not appear to be an excited and panicky hurry-up call for assistance, but will be welcomed as sane counsel from an old friend.

Using the Mails to Humanize Failure to Give Service

The greatest peril of the business man at a time of unusual prosperity is that his plant will be loaded to the point where it is impossible for him to give service.

If you receive orders for twice as many goods as you can ship within the time specified on your orders, you know that you must disappoint one-half of your customers, and that as a result of this disappointment, some of your customers are going to become dissatisfied. So in weathering the storm of prosperity, it is necessary once again to make use of the mails, to anticipate the complaints of the dealers by showing them in a very human way that the unexpected influx of orders has taxed capacity beyond its limits.

There is a tendency in prosperous times to call in salesmen, and call off advertising on the plea of, " We don't want any more orders." Your salesmen and your advertising, at this time, are the best friends that you have. You use them, not for the purpose of obtaining orders, but as a means of accomplishing the very things which you want to have done — re-establishment of goodwill with dealers who have become dissatisfied because of poor service.

Here again, the house which has established a regular means of communication with those who purchased from it, has a decided advantage over the house which has never previously used mail methods, because the goodwill messenger coming into the hands of the purchaser can very easily carry a message which will be read, believed, and understood. On the other hand, the house which has never sent out any mail advertising at any other time will, if it simply uses this means of getting out of a difficulty, most likely be regarded as an " excuse-maker."

An instance, which is rather out of the ordinary, indicates how one house met the situation of " too much prosperity."

It was at the time when everybody was buying all they could get. A certain manufacturing house was receiving orders from their dealers amounting to just about double what they could handle. They put the question squarely up to their dealers, pointing out that the size of the order received was far beyond what was usual and was therefore beyond their capacity to fill within the specified time. They told the dealers just exactly what they could do, and asked their consent to filling fifty per cent of the order and holding the balance of the order to be sent at a later date.

Most of the dealers saw the point and by anticipating the difficulty of filling orders, all received enough for their immediate needs, and were taken care of later on the balance of their orders without any disappointment.

Times of unusual prosperity like this are not very frequent, but, when they do arrive, the sales manager should be resourceful enough to take advantage of direct mail methods to keep his dealers satisfied, and his volume of orders well within his capacity to handle.

We have cited but a few of the common fundamentals in mail advertising which can be taken advantage of to regulate the market and stabilize business. These will show, however, the alert sales manager or business

executive how using the mails in his marketing methods gives him the ability to meet any
emergency, and to protect his business against
the ordinary fluctuations of markets and
buying conditions.

CHAPTER XI

ORGANIZED KNOWLEDGE IN MAIL SELLING

In no form of selling is the need for organized knowledge of greater importance than in marketing by mail. Mail advertising is no place for snap judgment. Guess-work should be eliminated by having plans based on fundamentals that experience has proven correct. Direct mail plans should harmonize with the sales department of the business and with the policy of the house, and be the product of the same thoughtful, deliberate judgment that governs the policies of accounting and administration.

The practical value of mail selling is being appreciated by an increasing number of firms and individuals in all lines of business every year, and while direct mail methods are widely used, yet they are also widely abused.

Because it is easy and inexpensive to reach prospects by mail, there has been a thoughtless tendency among the heads of business to attempt to attend to this department of their business themselves. These executives would not think of carrying on any of their other business operations without special preparation and careful training.

In many cases the mail advertising is entrusted to a subordinate, or to some clerk who divides his time between various clerical duties. In this case he not only lacks experience, but gives the advertising too little attention.

It is little wonder that mail advertising prepared by inexperienced people or not given suitable attention fails to produce the definite results that might reasonably be looked for.

Not only is the abuse of marketing methods by mail indulged in by business men who do not give the matter proper supervision, but there is a tendency for ambitious but inexperienced young men to pose as advertising experts.

Quite a number of these young fellows, who originate fine ideas, present clever illustrations, and write " snappy " copy, have succeeded in inducing business houses to buy their wares, and to send out circulars, broadsides, and other mailing pieces, which, because they have flattered the vanity of the advertiser, have been accepted.

It is a serious fallacy to jump at the conclusion that all that is necessary to do in order to sell goods by mail is to put together some nice illustrations and fine copy in an attractive piece of printing, and send out the circular to a list of prospective buyers. As a matter of fact the place for these features in any marketing by mail campaign is last instead of first. The essentials in any phase of marketing remain the same. Sales are only made by influencing people to buy. Whatever sales promotion method is undertaken must first of all have a practical merchandising basis, and the man who undertakes to prepare a mail campaign for any merchant must first of all have practical merchandising knowledge. He must be thoroughly familiar with all the intricate channels of trade. He should know the relation of cost to volume, know when the goods can be sold profitably and the price is right.

I have been asked time and again what qualifications are necessary for a man to possess who directs the work of marketing a product in whole or in part by mail. Here are the essential requirements, as I have found them out of an experience of twenty years' close application to this phase of merchandising.

1 A knowledge of the fundamentals of cost, accounting and finance.
2 A knowledge of marketing and merchandising, including a thorough understanding of the principles of mark-up and turnover.
3 A knowledge of advertising methods and the ability to prepare proper sales plans. An understanding of what can and cannot be accomplished with different types of mailing pieces to various groups of buyers.
4 A knowledge of what constitutes good copy, motives that make people buy, and an understanding of the human appeal in making a sale.

While I can find 99 applicants who have a pretty fair knowledge of numbers three and four, I cannot find one in a hundred who is well grounded in the principles embraced in numbers one and two. Right here is the out-standing weakness today among advertising men. The great majority think only in terms of the technical angle of advertising and not of the basic principles of economics and fundamentals of business.

Need for Analytical Minds

The first requisite of any marketing by mail campaign is an analysis of the facts in the case. These facts should be placed on paper in the form of an outline. The judgment of several experienced men is better than the judgment of any one man in deciding on sales plans and here we find the necessity for a keen analytical student — a man who has the capacity to inquire into facts and to select the right basis for the various sales appeals that are to be developed.

Such a man should be able to gather sales information together as a basis of the operation of a marketing by mail campaign. The facts must be known about the article to be sold, about the capacity of the firm selling the article, about its relative value as compared with others in the field: facts about the selling methods of competitors; facts about the ultimate market and how it is being reached.

Also facts about the middlemen or dealers and what connection has been formed between competitors' lines and their selling organizations; facts about dealer discounts; facts about territorial limitation; facts about transportation; facts about the response of the buyers to various types of appeals.

Very frequently, the stranger with an analytical mind, coming into a proposition of this kind, is able to inform the advertiser in regard to many features of his marketing which had never occurred to him before.

The fresh viewpoint often brings to life possibilities that the executive, close to his proposition, has failed to see.

The analytical mind is needed as a curb on the mind which sees purely from a sales standpoint and thinks only in terms of enthusiasm, and when the proposition is presented says: " Let's get out a broadside in colors." The analytical mind reasons on a basis of factory costs, and shows where it would be economically unprofitable to spend but a limited budget on a single advertising piece.

Where the enthusiastic mind would dictate:

" Let's broadcast this message all over the United States," the analytical mind shows that the appropriation necessary to do this is not available, and profitable results are secured by working more intensively in localities where better dealer distribution has been secured.

A manufacturer of farm lighting plants had been circularizing prospective dealers over the country for several years with fair results. A small corps of salesmen were employed to call on dealers and sell the local agencies. The few salesmen which the firm operated, however, were inadequate to cover the whole country and personal attention could be given by them only to prospects within a reasonable distance from their center of operation. They did considerable advertising in publications and direct by mail and received inquiries from dealers all over the country. Since their sales force was limited, it was only possible to follow up the dealers that were within the vicinity of the salesmen.

Such were the conditions when they appealed to an advertising analyst to outline mail sales promotion plans.

A zone was established covering only a few

states. The entire sales force was placed in this limited territory. Intensive mail advertising directed to this limited field produced inquiries which salesmen could at once follow up. The result of this intensive selling plan was the establishment of dealers at a very low cost and an increase in volume of sales.

The idea of the advertising to reach the dealers and produce the inquiries was given attention only after the conditions were arranged properly so as to enable the inquiries to be properly followed up.

In nearly every instance where our advertising counsel has been sought, we have been shown samples of the advertising previously turned out. In many cases, these are fine-looking pieces, and we do not wonder that they have met with the approval of the business executives if the sole standard of judgment was the fact that they were beautiful or interesting, because they are in many cases illustrated, well printed, and cleverly written.

But in many of the cases when we have said this much, we stated all that can be said in favor of the literature, because an analysis of the selling methods behind the efforts proved that the articles advertised were not presented in the light which was most likely to secure the coöperation of the buyer.

In many instances the mailings have been sent to a type of prospect who would not respond. In other cases the literature sent out had failed absolutely to interpret the human reaction of the prospective purchaser; quality was featured when comfort should have been played up; or price was stressed when time-saving should have been the strong point; or beauty was featured when utility should have been the point made. The advertisers had applied the wrong psychology in the matter of presentation.

Psychology is one of the things that people talk about and few people understand, but we all know that in order to induce any person to purchase, it is necessary to induce the individual to exercise his or her own desires and not the desires of the person writing the advertising copy. For this reason, the copy prepared by the inexperienced copy writer in the advertising field goes wide of the mark when it comes to producing maximum results in actual sales.

I do not know of any one single individual with ability and experience, no matter how unusual and extensive the ability and experience may be, who can compare in producing the results obtained by the harmonious coöperation of the various types of minds found in an organization planned to cover every phase of direct mail advertising.

Properly systemized libraries showing various types of advertising and listing the figures regarding various sales campaigns, letter tests, and other marketing by mail methods for ready reference are a very valuable part of an organization built to carry out effective direct advertising plans. These facts all contribute information which enables accurate and proper fundamentals to be determined as the basis for advertising campaigns.

It is impossible for the average advertising manager to collect facts and works of reference, and at the same time plan aggressive selling efforts. This is the job of the analyst.

The Place of Good Copy and Illustrations

Were we, however, to rely alone upon the student who will gather, collect, and correlate facts on merchandising, we would find that most of our sales campaigns would be dry and uninteresting. They would lack the selling touch, the enthusiasm, the " pep " and vim necessary to put things over. Enthusiasm is one of the main assets of the salesman, and should certainly be a part of every campaign intended to sell merchandise by mail. With the facts before us, showing clearly what the market is, what the appeal should be, who the prospects are, and other similar essential factors, the mind of a salesman is required to direct the production of the right sales presentation.

Here is where the advantage of a practical man, who goes out in the field and makes sales regularly every day, is of incalculable advantage in building up a plan for selling merchandise by mail. This salesman, the contact man, the man who comes personally in touch with the merchandiser is the ideal type of a man to direct the sales promotion plan after the facts have been gathered from the manufacturer about his product and the market to be reached.

Under the direction of the mail-salesman, layouts are prepared and copy written. It must have in it the spirit of salesmanship, and must pass the inspection of the practical salesman before it is submitted to the customer.

Good copy cannot be correctly judged by its literary merits. Some of the most ungrammatical things that ever were said produced fine selling results. Copy as prepared for the advertiser, should be the kind of copy that is human, that tells the prospect what he wants to know, that creates interest, desire and the impulse to act. It should be sane and sensible, not a clever aggregation of words, but the type of reasoning that brings conviction to the hearer and appeals to his desires.

I am a great believer in simplicity in the writing of mail advertising copy. Simplicity is the elimination of the nonessential in all things. It means survival, not of the fittest, but of the best. Simplicity cuts off waste and intensifies concentration. The simple type of copy makes it possible for mailings to produce actual sales.

The president of a large firm, doing an extensive business through the mails recently dictated the following paragraph to go to everyone in his office concerned in the preparation of literature and the writing of letters:

" Will you permit me to make a few suggestions as far as our literature and letters are concerned — call them ' rules ' if you want to:"

1. Use short words, and words which every reader can understand.

2. Make every sentence as direct and simple as possible. Avoid the inverted style, i. e., do not open with an explanatory clause.

3. Use many subheads, and make them helpful and attention compelling.

4. Keep the name of the product constantly before the reader — this even at the expense of what may seem to be, from a literary point of view, too much repetition.

5. Keep in mind the Sheldon rule that the first principle of salesmanship is first to attract attention. You ought to say the strongest thing you can at the very start — and then think of something stronger to say at the end — a " clincher."

6. Avoid exaggeration. Don't " gush." That doesn't mean weakness of state-

ment, because a simple fact may be stated in a very strong way.

7. Before you begin the preparation of literature, try to find out from the men in this office who know, what there is that is unique and different about it; then line up your selling talk and feature the "difference" strongly, so that it sticks right out in such a way as to hit the reader in the eye.

8. Somehow there should go into all our literature the carefully thought out suggestion that our products are more carefully made than those of most other houses and there is integrity back of them, and unusual scientific knowledge and technical skill.

9. Lose no opportunity to feature other of our products wherever you can do so properly, sometimes in the text, and nearly always somewhere on the circular itself.

10. Try to make every piece of literature valuable to the reader. It is valuable to the average man when it becomes helpful, i. e., contains suggestions

which he can use. It is not valuable to the average man when it simply becomes a matter of academic information.

11. I need say nothing about the importance of beauty, dignity and strength in the finished literature or letters. You all know the importance of these qualities.

Similarly the work of the illustrator must be under the direction and supervision of the salesman, because into the illustration must come that spirit of dramatization only a man who is full of enthusiasm and human sympathy can supply. There are various types of illustrators. If you will look through the directory under the heading of " artists " in a large city, you will find scores of names, and of those comparatively few can interpret in a humanly interesting way the sales message which the merchandiser wants to sell.

The ability to produce human interest illustrations makes an artist a specialist in that line and enables him to become a most valued part of any organization.

The same thought which an ordinary artist would portray in an ordinary picture becomes a vital, living thing, in the hands of an expert interpreter of the desires and sympathies of human nature, such as the advertising illustrator eventually becomes.

The Place for Mechanical Skill and Specialized Knowledge

One of the problems of the advertising manager who plans to get out a piece of advertising is not only to find a printer who knows how to do a fine job of printing but who also knows how to interpret advertising ideas. This type of printer will make the type lines conform to his ideas of harmony and balance, and give you correct printing interpretations of sales ideas that will sell twice as much merchandise for you.

For this reason, the value of a printer who understands how to make type talk, who will follow the instructions in regard to the right headings to emphasize, and other features that put the real selling punch into any piece of printed matter is almost incalculable.

The special knowledge of the man who understands inks, and knows the relationship of color and its attractiveness, who has studied his profession from the standpoint of advertising so that he may make every piece of work which goes through his hands of increased advertising value is another indispensable feature of well-planned mail merchandising material.

Similarly, through every operation, the need for specialized knowledge is evident. The man who selects the list, who simply has so many names of so many people of a certain classification, cannot give you the intelligent service of the man who is trained to look at his problems from the viewpoint of selling possibilities.

The Need for Accurate Postal Information

One of the most important phases of direct mail advertising is the need of accurate postal information. Many advertising campaigns have been prepared and all details perfected, only to find that when they reached the mailing room they were too heavy to be mailed at the expected rate. Many of them have been sent to the post office and returned because the postage was insufficient.

Many people expect an accurate check on

their mailing and yet when they send out their mailing pieces under first class mail, there is no responsibility on the part of the post office to return undelivered mail unless the words " Return Postage Guaranteed " are printed on the face of the mailing.

Other people make the mistake of printing pieces of a wrong size so that they become mutilated when handled by the mail-carrier. Others send out post cards and folders which do not conform to the postal regulations and reduce the returns that should be expected.

These, and other mistakes, which occur from a lack of knowledge of postal regulations show that the assistance and coöperation of a department whose business it is to specialize on postal knowledge is a very necessary part of a well-planned campaign of merchandising by mail.

The same great business truth applies in the case of merchandising by mail as in nearly every other field of endeavor.

If one man would undertake to build an automobile by himself, he could probably get through, but it would be a genius indeed who would be equipped with the necessary knowledge of the proper treatment of metals,

the principles of combustion, electric generation, the laws of balance, the skill of wood-
working, of upholstering, and the many other
things which enter into the making of a motor
car.

We are all prepared to admit the service of
an organization of coöperating experts, each
one concentrating on his own particular field,
produces a much better product at a much
lower price than the one which the individual
could be expected to produce working alone.

This principle is carried through even in
the smallest of our needs. We find that shoes
are better and more economically made by
having one man make the soles, another man
make the heels, another man make the de-
signs, another man make the uppers, and
another corps of specialists to put all of those
things together.

Specialized knowledge combined in a co-
operating organization has been the answer
to economic and satisfactory production. The
same principle applies to service organizations — a band of specialists can do more
thorough and more systematic work than any
one individual no matter how clever he may
be.

The purpose of this chapter is to show that the business man who relies on any one not equipped with the necessary experience to carry out his advertising schedule, is working at a great disadvantage when it is possible for him to obtain the services of an organization of experts to carry out complete advertising plans with the thoroughness impossible to the individual even when an expert.

You would not entrust a slightly experienced assistant with the task of decorating the office because you know you would get a result which would not be a credit to the organization. How much more important it is that your advertising work, which involves the psychology of influencing the minds of those people on whom your business depends — the customer who must buy from you — should be entrusted to the best skill you can obtain.

Because merchandising by mail is a science involving all the skill of the advertiser, all of the ingenuity of the correspondent, all of the ability of the personal salesman, and all of the skill of the business manager, it is vitally important that the work of preparing merchandising campaigns by mail be placed in the hands of people whose ability and experience will keep you away from pitfalls, and produce results of which you will be warranted in having pride.

It is safe to say that over eighty per cent of the mail matter sent out in the United States finds its way to the wastebasket, and the reason is largely because the work of the preparation of this mail matter has been entrusted to those with no special skill, no technical training, and in many cases no aptitude for the work they are attempting to do.

It is about time that the business men of America woke up to this great waste which is going on — this drain on their resources — the sending out of ineffective, poorly planned mail advertising pieces.

Remember, you are merchandising when you send out a business communication through the mail, and if it is poorly addressed, ludicrous, or has an unfortunate, unsightly appearance, or lacks ability to inspire confidence, you cannot expect any better sales results than if you sent out a salesman who exhibited no knowledge of the goods he was trying to sell, and who had no aptitude or training for salesmanship.

The most successful businesses in the United States are those who have the best trained salesmen. These same institutions recognize this principle in making sales, and their merchandising through the mail is carried on with the same regard for skillful presentation as are their sales efforts.

CHAPTER XII

THE CASH VALUE OF MAILING LISTS

If there is any one thing of vital importance in a plan of merchandising by mail it is the quality of the mailing list to be used. It is not a question of how many thousand names there are on the list, but whether they are actual potential prospects is what counts.

Many people think they are getting a bargain when they buy stock lists containing thousands of names at a low price. As a matter of fact, the first cost of the list is a very small part of the expense. Every time unnecessary names are used the cost in postage alone is far more than the original cost of the list.

Only by constant revision and eternal vigilance do reputable list houses of the country succeed in eliminating " dead " names and giving to their clients a list in which the element of waste has been taken out.

I once talked with a well-known manufacturer who had become discouraged over his efforts to sell by mail.

Investigation showed that he had been sending advertising out at regular intervals, but results were not satisfactory.

The first thought was that his advertising was of the wrong kind, and he was surprised when the major part of it was given an O. K. by the merchandising man who made the investigation.

" But that literature hasn't been bringing me results," he said. " How do you figure it can be used profitably again?" " By sending it to a good list," was the response.

His poor list was displaced by a carefully prepared list of customers and prospective customers. Compared to the old list there was only twenty-five per cent duplications. Many of the names on the new lists were prospects who had been entirely overlooked by this manufacturer.

The campaign sent to the new list produced excellent returns in percentage of inquiries and mail orders. Sales methods turned a large per cent of the inquiries into new customers and profitable business.

IMPORTANCE OF MAILING LIST SHOWN BY DIAGRAM

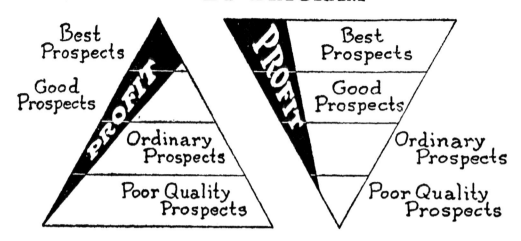

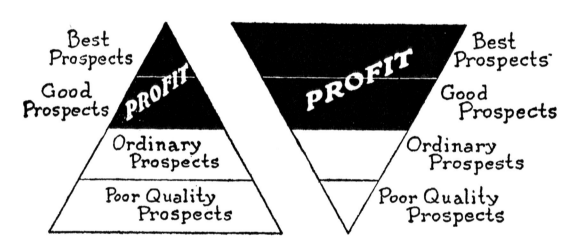

It is poor policy to work medium or low-grade prospects in sales efforts before all of the best prospective customers have been thoroughly covered.

This diagram indicates ordinary distribution of effort in class of names in an average mailing list. The average run of prospective customers does not yield highest percentage of profits because a large proportion are medium and low-grade prospects.

The black shows how efforts should be concentrated on the best prospects. It yields a larger percentage of results and profits.

The results of merchandising by mail depend upon the value and accuracy of the mailing list to which the literature is sent.

To those who have never used mail methods of marketing, it might appear that a list is of little consequence. You sometimes hear inexperienced advertisers say: " Oh, we can easily get a list of names." That is very true. It is very easy to get a list of names, just as it is very easy to meet people, but just the same as it is necessary for a personal salesman to select the firms and individuals upon whom he makes his calls, so it is necessary for the person merchandising by mail to select very carefully the people to whom he shall send his messages through the mail.

If a salesman does not exercise care in selecting the character of the house upon whom he calls, he will find that most of his time is wasted looking for the right prospects. Possibly only one out of every ten people called on will be prospects and give him attention.

The man who works in this way, with only ten per cent of his time devoted to selling, and ninety per cent devoted to finding prospects, will necessarily have to content himself with a very small volume of sales. Likewise, the man who uses a list which is not carefully selected, where only one-tenth of the people to whom he mails his literature are actual prospective purchasers, will find that his cost of mailing bears such a high figure in relation to the volume of sales produced, that the cost of doing business in this way is prohibitive. Even though the list be of a fairly good grade the number of names one can select as prospects for sales is limited in many ways.

For instance prospects for the sale of the Rolls-Royce car are limited to the very wealthy people of the United States, and any appeal made to the 110,000,000 will find a wastage of over 109,500,000, because the people in this country earning $10,000 a year or more, according to the tax schedule of 1923, are limited to 223,906.

If a concern has an article which will sell to people earning from $3000 to $10,000 it will have a market of 1,792,500, according to the same tax schedule. An article which will sell to people earning over $1000 a year would command a market of over 7,000,000. This is also according to the same tax schedule.

If a device can be sold in every home, there

are 24,000,000 homes in the United States. If it is a device for every automobile owner, there are, according to the latest count, somewhere between 11,000,000 and 12,000,000 automobiles. On the other hand, if the product is something which can be sold to tanners only, there are fewer than 700 tanneries in the United States, and other industries show even a smaller number. Some of the lists are difficult to obtain. Others are apparently readily available from such sources as the classified section of the telephone directories, etc.

Mortality of Different Lists

The mortality of names is high in a telephone directory. The experience of the Chicago Telephone Company shows that the changes necessary in its telephone book amount to twenty-two per cent every year.

Let us suppose that you take a book a year old and address and send out a 10,000 mailing, the thousands of letters that you would get from the dead-letter office would be astonishing.

However, the people whose names appear in the telephone book are no more subject to death, or bankruptcy, or change of location than any other variety of people. So it is no wonder that the business house which has not revised its mailing list for two or three years becomes annoyed at the tremendous volume of returned mail. In a list of barbers there are thirty per cent changes a year; there is a twenty-five per cent mortality in school teachers; there are 6000 changes every day among concerns listed in Dun's and Bradstreet's Rating Books.

When several years ago, our firm conducted complete revisions of lists for one firm we found the following depreciation in the various classifications.

Householders ....22 per cent changes in one year
Dealers ....23 " " " " " "
Barbers ....30 " " " " " "
Agents ....29 " " " " " "
Advertising Men.37 " " " " " "

Other tests which have been made from time to time in recent years proved a similar high mortality.

The average mailing piece costs about six cents to produce and get ready for the mails and two cents postage so that one-fourth of your total expense is required for postage. You add to this 1½ cents for addressing the envelope and filling in the name on the letter, and you have 3½ cents out of eight cents which is saved whenever a " dead name " is taken off the mailing schedule, so that a correct mailing list is worth almost half of the total direct mail appropriation.

One of the large retail stores in Chicago had a list of 35,000 charge customers, accumulated over a period of ten or more years. It was the intention of this firm to circularize that list as it stood. They were, however, prevailed on to have the list revised and it was found that over half of the names were inaccurate. This meant that to mail to this list under one cent postage $175.00 would have been thrown away. A two-cent mailing to the same list would be a postage loss of $350.00. In addition there would have been a tremendous waste of material, and time for the printing, and preparation.

The experience of a Philadelphia concern shows a list of 1,000 names used for a period of three years, will have sustained the following casualties:

410 people will have changed addresses one to four times

261 will have moved to parts unknown

124 will have already bought

83 will have bought a competing article

7 will have died

1 will have gone to jail

A total of 886 persons out of every thousand or practically ninety per cent of this antiquated list were absolutely useless names. That is, for every dollar spent mailing to this list 90 cents was thrown away.

Direct mail advertising sent to a list of this kind is largely money needlessly wasted. It is just as logical to expect a worthless list to bring results as it is to expect a leaky bucket with eight or ten holes in it to keep afloat on the surface of the water for any appreciable length of time.

What merchant would knowingly enter into any plan of marketing where he knew that practically one half of his effort was completely wasted, and what man would consider himself a merchant, who would deliberately make sales efforts to produce business from men who were dead or who had moved away? And yet this is just exactly what the merchant does who uses an old mailing list, where a large percentage of his expenditure goes to people who are no longer in existence.

When the high mortality of such mailing lists is compared with the guarantee given by most reputable mailing list houses — guarantees of ninety per cent, ninety-five per cent and ninety-eight per cent — you will realize the intense application these houses make on the matter of eliminating waste material.

Sub-Dividing Lists and a Master List

Even with the compilation of the lists properly attended to, many merchants fail of their real opportunity by sending indiscriminately all of their advertising matter to their complete list of prospects.

Obviously, all merchandise sold by a department store, for instance, is not purchased by the same individual. The person who buys an ash sifter is not very likely to buy a $3000 Oriental rug, and the woman who buys a dress in the basement for $5.98 is not likely to be in the market for a $1,000 set of furs.

Many manufacturers sell part of their products to one industry, and part to another, and if they only have a general list, a large part of every mail must, of necessity, be wasted.

In conducting a campaign for a manufacturer of a product selling to ice cream manufacturers, druggists, and high class hotels, we found that they had a mailing list of about 24,000 names; also that they had been sending out to the hotel owners and the ice cream manufacturers mailings intended only for the drug stores, and the drug store would receive mailings intended only for the hotel keeper. The hotel keeper would similarly receive mailings intended for the ice cream manufacturer.

One of the first recommendations we made was for the subdivision of the list so that mailings intended for the drug stores would be sent to this list only, and mailings intended for the hotels would be sent to hotel men only.

"But," was the objection, "if we divide our list this way, it will be necessary to look through three different lists in order to find a customer's record as soon as an order is received."

The very simple and obvious thing which had not occurred to them, and which had been their only reason heretofore for not subdividing the list, was the matter of compiling a master list for reference on the receipt of orders, and keeping the subdivided list for the mailing purposes only.

The master list immediately identified the division in which the right card could be found so that a prospect could be changed from prospect to customer as soon as an order was received. Furthermore, the subdivided list effected savings in printer's bills, addressing costs, and postage, which in a very short time, paid for the entire work of compilation and checking the old list and compiling the master list.

Quite apart from its economic value, the psychology of sending the wrong type of advertising to any prospect must immediately be apparent: The hotel man being told how a drug store profits by using a certain article feels that the company addressing him does not know in what business he is engaged. When he does receive advertising applying only to hotel men, he will remember the previous lack of directness of the advertising of this company, and will not regard them as good business men to the same extent that he would if every communication addressed to

him were on the particular topic in which he
was interested.

With subdivided lists, constantly re-
checked for changes in address, death, etc.,
the merchant contemplating marketing by
mail, has the groundwork for a splendid business because he can make his moves count
with telling effect and secure a much larger
percentage of returns than if he is addressing
a miscellaneous list where only a few people
are vitally interested.

Building Mailing Lists

There are many desirable lists which cannot be supplied from any known sources of
information but which must be compiled as
a result of special effort applied in this direction.

Many concerns build up their mailing lists
from the replies to advertisements in magazines. In this way they can discriminate
between the different types of individuals.

The sale of books has been very effectively
promoted by advertisements which would
draw replies from people who were interested
in a particular subject. Some inexpensive

treatise is mailed free, and then the name is put on the books for a genuine, systematic campaign.

Special lists are sometimes built up as a result of direct mail inquiries. In building up a list in this way, a questionnaire is first sent out to the list of names which offers the greatest likelihood of potential prospects, and from the answers to this questionnaire, the list of those actually in the market for a particular device is readily attained.

Other lists are only obtained as a result of personal information. There are many houses who make personal investigations of the field. That is to say, if they want to find out who is the leading hardware man in every town in the country, their salesmen who make these towns are instructed to make inquiries in each town to find out who is the leading hardware dealer.

From the information sent in by the salesmen, a direct mail campaign is prepared, and the interest of the hardware dealer is secured to act as representative. After the campaign has done its work of education the salesman goes back on the job and completes the sale.

Some people make use of the expedient of

using other people's salesmen to supply them with information by offering a certain amount for each name an individual sends in. For instance, the maker of a new type of paper for use in adding machines might want to find out the name of every person in the town using an adding machine. Without going to the expense of sending his salesmen, he could have the salesmen of an adding machine company calling on these prospects furnish the names for him. Others build up a list much more quickly by sending out a questionnaire.

Many salesmen who find it difficult to call on " cold " leads make their first trip into the territory one of investigation, and when they find out the people who are the logical prospects for their line, they send back the names to the home office. The home office then sends the literature which introduces the merchandise to the prospective buyer, and the salesman when he makes his second trip does so with the advantage of the advertising matter preceding him.

These various methods for obtaining lists (some at an expense amounting to about $25 a name) show the value placed on a live list of prospects by merchandisers who have a worthy article to sell.

How Reputable List Houses Anticipate Your Needs

While it is possible to build up excellent lists in the manner described, a great many lists which have been compiled as a result of rather extensive questionnaires or from the calls of personal salesmen, or other methods, at great expense, could have been obtained from a list house in a fraction of the time and cost had facilities of the house been known.

Not very long ago, a man who had planned a small special mailing came to see us. Prior to coming, he had sent in asking for a list of boat builders, and to this list he had sent out an inquiry asking how many of them manufactured motor boats. He came back to us with replies from 117, and was astonished to learn that he could have saved all of this expense by simply buying our list of motor boat builders which showed 229 manufacturers.

Another concern, interested in selling a coal saving device, sent out men especially throughout the country to put down the names of manufacturers with large plants. After spending hundreds of dollars in this way, they were surprised to learn that we could supply them from our records with the names of manufacturers of any rating desired which identically covered their needs.

There is a surprising lack of knowledge of the facilities for doing direct mail work, probably because this is a new profession which business men have not begun to fully appreciate and possibly because the things accomplished in the direct mail field seem impossible to the uninitiated. Nearly every phase of human endeavor has been classified and listed. Almost any type of prospect can be obtained from sources which are readily available.

Such classification has been the natural outcome of thousands of inquiries for specialized lists, so that today classification of more than 6,000 different divisions of buyers is available. Whether the manufacturer wants to reach the eleven manufacturers of aeroplane hangars in the United States, or the 148,097 general stores, or any other classifications, taken by industry, rating or locality, he finds the information already gathered for him, and the list available for his immediate use.

Many ways and means have been devised to systematically correct the list. The plan of simply dropping the names of customers who have not ordered for a certain period is unsatisfactory because the name of a logical prospect might be eliminated. The prospect might, if retained on the list, send in a large order that would more than compensate the manufacturer for the expense of an entire mailing.

It is not unusual for an advertiser to enclose a post card with house organs or other literature, reading in effect: " Shall we continue or discontinue sending you our literature? " All who do not return the cards may be regarded as indifferent and subject for removal from the list.

Another method is to send out a postcard on which wording to this effect appears: " On (insert date) we will discontinue sending you literature unless advised to the contrary."

This brings response from a varying per cent of the list. However, many manufacturers do not remove the names from the list if they do not reply, as to do so would be to adopt too arbitrary and radical a policy. Some advertisers enclose a stamped return envelope as an incentive to a reply and this undoubtedly has some effect in bringing back requests to continue their names on the list or to discontinue them.

One manufacturer sends a first class letter to his house organ list every six months, with stamped return envelope and slip, requesting information as to whether the prospects desire to be continued on the list.

An effective plan is to send out a notice forcing prospects and customers to indicate their interest by checking the literature they are interested in. Such a form reads: " Owing to the cost of publication, we will not send our catalog to any person who fails to fill out the blank form below. If you desire this catalog please sign this card and return it or indicate your interest otherwise."

Every advertiser should constantly follow a plan for keeping his mailing list up to date and ridding himself of the expense of paying for advertising which is sent out without profitable returns.

CHAPTER XIII

THE RELATION OF PUBLICITY TO SELLING BY MAIL

One of the common faults of advertisers today is that they engage in campaigns of advertising to accomplish desired results when analysis would show the plan being followed would have no possible chance of being successful, because the kind of advertising being used could never produce the desired results.

Every medium of advertising is good when properly applied, but for real results the kind of advertising best fitted to the particular problem should be chosen. It may be a catalog sent out in mail order style. It may be national mail order advertising, or national dealer advertising. It may be national consumer advertising or it may be the circularizing of lists for inquiries or orders. It may be " coupling-up " advertising by mail to dealers to increase the effectiveness of trade paper or national advertising. It may be direct advertising to selected lists, or in limited territory operations, for the featuring of a problem where secrecy is imperative.

Sometimes we see one kind of advertising denounced as a failure. This is unjust to that kind of advertising and utterly absurd. That fault is not usually with the method but with the person who forced the method to be used. Analysis will show the proper channels of advertising that should bring success. That is why every sales problem should be carefully analyzed and the marketing methods that are best fitted should be chosen.

In this connection the following instance is cited: A manufacturer of a high quality automobile tire came into our office for counsel. He was very much discouraged over the results he had received from national advertising. He had spent thousands of dollars for seven pages of advertising in the *Saturday Evening Post*. The advertisements were handsomely designed and well written. The illustrations were produced in colors. The combination formed just the type of advertising to build prestige for any automobile tire. However, results in sales proved disappointing.

We asked him certain pertinent questions designed to give us information regarding his company. His tire was manufactured in Massachusetts and he had built up quite a large local demand by personal effort. He had a few dealers but they were located in New England only. Wherever he had dealers he had found that the *Post* advertising had helped sales. In other sections of the country where he had no dealers the results were zero.

His attitude was that national advertising was a failure and he was fully resolved to discontinue that type of advertising and sell his product direct by mail.

The case just cited is typical of many others where advertising, because of lack of success, is condemned. In many instances the fault lies, as in this case, not in the advertising but in the method of its use.

In the case of the tire manufacturer, dealers had to be established over a more extensive area. Direct mail was used to help establish them. Personal salesmen reached the larger cities. Advertising and publicity of other forms established desire in territories where salesmen were not calling.

There is no denying the fact that national

advertising is a far-reaching potential factor in making sales to the mass of consumers, or the fact that trade paper advertising is an excellent medium of publicity in problems where the trade must be influenced. But to rely on publicity of any one kind to complete the merchandising circle is as illogical as limiting your articles of dress to a pair of trousers and a coat.

When it comes to the problem of merchandising, very few men apply the same common sense that they do when it comes to selecting factory equipment, or determining the policies that will govern their selling through men.

It is very necessary in considering the subject of merchandising by mail that we give a great deal of thought to the part which publicity plays.

It would be foolish to try to disguise the fact that the salesman finds it much easier to sell dealers nationally advertised brands. It would be equally foolish to deny that the sales message through the mail makes it much easier to market the goods advertised.

Just as the salesman, representing the house whose prestige has been developed by liberal trade-paper advertising, finds a receptive audience, so the mail message is more likely to receive attention when it comes from a house whose prestige has been established by trade-paper advertising.

Co-ordination of General and Dealer Advertising

A manufacturer of food products, selling through dealers, had consulted with an advertising agency which advised him to spend $50,000 in national advertising to popularize his line. He was not satisfied that this was the proper way to merchandise his product and he had thought seriously about adopting mail methods as the proper channel of distribution. He had read somewhere of the success of Butler Brothers in merchandising their wares to dealers direct by mail. He came to us fully convinced that direct mail was the method which he should follow in merchandising his food products to dealers.

This man could see very clearly that no matter how extensively goods were advertised to the public, unless the public was given an opportunity to buy by seeing the goods displayed in the dealer's store, the chances for a sale would be very slim. He could see, on the other hand, that if he could get his article on the shelves of the dealers, with appropriate window and store displays, sales could be made even without the assistance of national advertising.

We pointed out to him the difficulty of getting dealers to accept a product which was unknown, and which had not been advertised to the public. The dealer is not anxious to obtain goods to put on his shelves, but he is anxious to have the sales which result because of public demand.

This particular manufacturer had an appropriation of $50,000 to spend. His agency had recommended that he spend his whole appropriation in national advertising, not providing any way for the establishment of dealers.

This man himself was anxious to secure dealer distribution and was unsold on the value of national advertising because he considered this advertising agency's recommendation a one-sided affair, which did not provide a complete merchandising plan for him. The only way we could convince him of the proper method of handling his sales problem was to recommend tests, and in this way prove that the plans we suggested would produce for him.

The first test was made by mail to a list of 5,000 grocers, offering the line of food products, together with direct mail selling helps, window and counter displays. From this mailing only twenty-five acceptances were received.

The second test was also made by mail in conjunction with a national advertising campaign, and spoke of the consumer demand resulting from this national campaign. From this second test, also to a 5,000 list, one hundred seventy-eight dealers were lined up. The value of national advertising in this case had been clearly demonstrated and in coöperation with the direct mail selling plan shown to be of great value.

Another case, which in its first aspect was similar to the one just cited, proved to be entirely different in the results obtained.

A furnace manufacturer came to us very much enthused with the results to be obtained from national advertising. He wanted to place most of his budget in national advertising and only a very nominal sum in direct mail advertising. A consultation showed that his selling territory was limited because of high transportation charges and also keen competition in certain fields.

We recommended a direct mail campaign to consumers in conjunction with his merchandising by mail. He decided, however, to make tests for himself.

By counsel along these lines, showing how, when and where to use each type of sales effort, confidence in advertising and sane policies of merchandising were once more restored.

It is not unusual to have people come to us and say:

"We are spending $50,000 a year in national advertising, and we have decided to eliminate this and put the money in direct mail advertising."

Others have taken the same view in regard to their appropriation for trade paper advertising, or for other forms of publicity.

Their dominant thought is to effect a change of policy in the hope that the change will demonstrate a better selling method.

Importance of Deciding Policy

This is a blind, unreasonable policy that is a serious menace. It frequently is stepping out of the frying pan into the fire, and it is absolutely unnecessary.

It may be true in some cases that national advertising is the thing that is needed. It may be true that advertising in trade papers is the thing which is desirable. It may be true, in other cases, that the national advertising has been a mistake, and that it should be replaced by direct mail.

In most propositions where the ultimate appeal is to the masses, national advertising influence has a splendid influence on sales and often is the most economical way of building up demand from the consumer.

In many cases the effort of trade paper advertising is such as to make this kind of advertising especially attractive.

In other cases direct advertising to segregated lists of prospects is the most desirable type of publicity for developing volume of business at minimum cost.

There is no cut and dried rule that can be applied to meet all conditions made. What is medicine in one case will be poison to another. That is why I emphasized to the manufacturer the vital need of experienced counsel behind every advertising campaign in order that the advertiser can most surely base his policy on a stable foundation that will lead to successful results.

The first year he used national advertising, obtaining his dealers direct by mail. The results were quite a large number of dealers (630) but a total sales volume of only $87,-000. Of this amount $53,000 was in the territory we had outlined as his logical market, and only $35,000 in all the other territory, where more than three-fourths of his new dealers were. These unsatisfactory sales soon caused a mortality in the number of dealers. The sales expense this first year amounted to $72,000.

The following year he adopted our suggestion and concentrated on certain territory only. He used direct mail both to present his offer to dealers and also to advertise his line to prospective consumers. The result was the building up of his dealer representation in this territory from one hundred forty-eight to three hundred two, and an increase in sales from $53,000 in this territory to $287,000.

The reason for the difference in these two marketing problems is readily apparent when we consider where the incentive to buy originates. The decision to buy foodstuffs is made by the woman who reads national advertising, but furnaces are generally sold to men who are largely influenced by the reputation of the local dealer. In one case national advertising was necessary, but in the other case direct mail advertising was the only means of making use of the reputation of the local dealer.

The reputable advertising agency recognizes the importance of direct mail advertising in any product sold through dealers and will advise a reasonable amount of a firm's advertising appropriation for direct mail methods. Many of the most successful agencies appreciate the value of specialized direct mail counsel and production methods to such an extent that they call us in to counsel or advise their clients to operate their direct mail plans through our organization. In cases where they fail to see the necessity for this part of the merchandising campaign they frequently lose the account altogether.

The policy of the most successful agencies was well brought out at the convention of the

Advertising Clubs of the World at Atlantic City in a talk by H. B. Le Quatte, who supervises the advertising for the Boston Woven Hose and Rubber Company.

It has always been the policy of this concern to divide the appropriations in all cases where the ultimate sales are made through dealers on a fifty-fifty basis — for every dollar spent for national publicity to influence the consumer, a dollar is spent in " hooking up " with the dealer — telling him of the plans and inducing him to coöperate.

Their Boston Woven Hose campaigns have been extremely successful, having built up in nine years a goodwill that is valued at $3,000,000 for an advertising expense of $276,-000. The same policy is applied to all accounts handled by this agency, where the product is sold through dealers. This policy of merchandising the national advertising to dealers by mail is undoubtedly responsible for the many extraordinary successes cited by that speaker.

While the plan of national advertising merchandised to dealers by mail is extremely effective, the Boston Woven Hose and Rubber Company carried the idea of intensive selling further. They took a limited section, a territory around Chicago, in a five hundred mile radius, and put $15,000 into newspapers and $15,000 into merchandising that newspaper advertising.

After the season had closed, a check up of the entire country was made. They took the increase that had been made in the territory around Chicago, deducting first the general increase. They found that the Chicago territory showed an increase of one hundred forty-three per cent while the country generally showed an increase of forty per cent to fifty per cent. The $30,000 which they put into newspaper and direct mail advertising came back the first year. Both the agency and the manufacturer believe that this would have been impossible with consumer advertising alone, or without the merchandising of the advertising by mail.

Where Trade Papers Are Used to Establish Prestige

Class circulation, the reaching of men engaged in any particular trade, profession, or calling, has been developed to a very high plane by the trade papers of the United States. There are, of course, good and bad advertising mediums in all of these fields, and the buying potentiality of the subscribers differs very widely in the different classes of publications.

Such publications as *Motor Boating* which goes to motor boat users might almost be considered national advertising, and it is very probable that papers of this type are a fine medium for selling direct to the consumer, but the great majority of the trade papers are those such as the *Dry Goods Reporter,* whose circulation is confined to dry goods dealers, and the value of whose advertising columns is largely based on prestige.

While sales are largely made to dealers as the result of this trade paper advertising, very little of it can be keyed so that the direct sales results are seldom traceable. For this reason, we frequently find that the people become dissatisfied with their appropriations for trade paper advertising.

In many cases the retailer who subscribes for a trade paper is too busy to devote much time to reading the magazine delivered to him, and it lies on his desk until the arrival of the following month's magazine. There are retailers, moreover, who are interested in picking up the magazine and looking through it for important features. They frequently refer to the magazine when they want the name of some particular advertiser, and if care is taken in the preparation of the advertising that goes into the trade paper, it will at least have left its impression on the subscriber's mind so that when the name is presented in a definite selling effort, the prestige of the magazine will be remembered.

Where the product is one that must be sold through dealers and the particular type of dealer handling the line is a reader of trade magazines, the advertising appropriation for this purpose is well spent.

It is an excellent plan to conduct a mail campaign to dealers in addition to trade paper advertising, calling attention to the trade paper ads., showing proofs of national and trade paper advertisements, thus assuring that the dealers are kept cognizant of what is being done. The result of this policy is invariably advantageous and a wiser investment than depending on the influence of trade paper publicity alone.

A plan for merchandising by mail is invariably advantageous and a wiser investment than depending on the influence of trade paper publicity alone.

A consistent plan of merchandising by mail will certainly be much more successful if it takes advantage of every good means of getting the article to the attention of the purchaser, and the trade paper is one of the recognized means of promoting goodwill for merchandise as well as establishing the prestige of the house.

What the trade paper does not do, however, is to present a personalized message, delivered to the desk of the proper executive in a manner which he cannot overlook because it is not surrounded by other factors of interest. This can be accomplished alone by direct mail.

Billings and Spencer, manufacturers of drop forgings and small tools selling through jobbers, had advertised for many years through trade papers, and prior to 1920 had done institutional advertising in the *Saturday Evening Post,* spending $80,000 a year. Results were unknown. Their salesmen called on the jobbing trade only. They decided in

1921 to test out the plan of promoting sales by mail and through newspapers, and to do this selected four localities for the tryout. An appropriation of $5,000 was set aside for this purpose and a direct mail campaign launched in New York, Cleveland, Kansas City and Detroit. Results in these localities showed twenty-eight per cent increase in sales.

Half of the business done before this campaign was in drop forgings; tools and machinery made up the other half. After the campaign on small tools, the largest volume of business was in tools.

This again illustrated the advantage of combining newspaper and direct mail intensively in selected localities rather than depending on national or trade paper advertising unsupported by aggressive " tie up " sales methods.

How Billboards Help Mail Selling Produce Greatest Results

A druggist in Chicago came to us for merchandising counsel in connection with billboard advertising. He told us that a few months previous he had been advised to go into an advertising campaign, and had spent $20,000 in billboard and street car publicity which had failed to produce any results.

Here was another case of a one-sided appropriation which had made the user of this type of publicity sour on the thing he had been sold too much of. Whoever had given him the foolish advice to spend this much money without any backing up of distribution, or newspaper, or magazine advertising had actually injured their own case. If a well rounded out merchandising plan had been laid out for this advertiser he would have been able to appreciate the logical place for billboard and street car signs, and they would have formed a permanent part of his appropriation in all future campaigns.

National advertising campaigns without dealer distribution must fail. Newspaper advertising must fail for the same reason. Billboard advertising without any connection between itself and the sale is of absolutely no value. A direct mail campaign will fail of its best results without the support of other phases of selling.

A few years ago a coal jobber, who was acting as representative for one of the high grade Illinois coals, used a direct mail campaign to popularize this particular grade.

The first step in the campaign was a series of mailing pieces to the coal dealers in the district where industrial plants were located.

This series of mailing pieces educated the executives on the heat value of a certain brand of coal.

As soon as the second piece of the campaign had been sent out, there appeared advertisements in the newspapers emphasizing these same features, and displaying the trademark name of the coal.

These advertisements were presented in attractive form with strong human interest copy and good illustrations.

At the same time billboard space had been provided in well selected locations where the executives of the large industrial plants in such regions as the central manufacturing district could see them on their approach to business, going to and from lunch, and again at night.

The combination secured a continual reminder, in his morning paper, on the way to work, on his desk at the office, three times during the day on billboards, and then in the

evening paper at night, which proved to be a
very effective way of overcoming the business
executive's indifference, and the number of
telephone calls which resulted from this campaign showed the success of this type of merchandising.

To make an intelligent selection of a plan
for merchandising, all of these factors should
be considered. The value of publicity of any
kind should not be overlooked because publicity is one of the fine points of merchandising which is but very little understood.

Using Publicity to Coöperate in Limited Territory

One of the problems with which we are most
frequently confronted is that of the man who
is limited, by keen competition, by transportation difficulties, or by financial or factory
capacity in the territory which he can cover
with his merchandise.

While no rule can be laid down to apply to
all cases, it is usually the wisest business
course where any limitation is required, to
limit the territory, rather than to limit the
intensity of a campaign.

If an appropriation must necessarily be small, it is far better to cover one state and use all methods of publicity in that state, and sell intensively and build up a local demand before reaching out into greater territory.

Very logically, a campaign of this kind must omit, for the time being at least, the use of national publicity because the cost of national publicity is too great to allow a waste of circulation in forty-seven states, and reap the publicity advantage of only one state.

To make up this lack of national publicity, it is necessary to intensify the other sales campaigns. Use more liberally local newspaper advertising, and use a more intensified direct mail campaign. Make use of billboards and street car cards more extensively, and take advantage as largely as possible of window signs and counter displays in the store itself.

Even when the product has been found to be one fitted for mail order selling, it is far better to limit the sales territory to one state, rather than to reduce the number of mailing pieces, because very frequently five pieces sent to a 10,000 list will be far more effective than a single piece sent to a 50,000 list. By taking advantage of repetition, we increase the sales influence of our advertising. This is one of the principles of advertising that is too little understood.

CHAPTER XIV

USING THE MAILS TO KEEP CUSTOMERS SOLD

This is the day of turnover.

One hears much of the necessity of securing a rapid turnover of stock on hand; also the evil of labor turnover and the constant trouble in the breaking in of inexperienced help.

There is another kind of turnover, however, which is frequently lost sight of when business is good and sales volume remains constant or is increasing — that is customer turnover.

In these days of the persistent search for new business, both by advertising and personal solicitation, the old customers who have ridden along with the firm through good times and bad are sometimes lost sight of.

It is, no doubt, a pleasant feeling to look over the month's or the year's sales and see an increase, but it is well not to forget that

Mail Orders
help
Turnover

The average retailer is a poor mail order man. During the next few years — if he is going to survive — he must become a good mail order man. In addition to his regular selling, he will sell by mail.

It is my opinion that the retailer will also buy more and more by mail.

Why?

Because after the initial stock order is received and sales are made, the wide-awake merchant will keep a record of sales and at each week-end will reorder to fill in stock.

This means that stocks will be kept up and investments kept down. It means a sure check on slow sellers and more intelligence in getting turnover on the quick-selling goods.

Turnover means profit!

this increase may be partly due to seasonal changes or improved conditions in your locality or some other factor for which you cannot rightly take credit.

Before you throw your elbow out of joint trying to pat yourself on the back, just go to the ledger and see if your old friends are still buying from you, the people who helped you when you needed their business ten years or five years ago.

If they continue with the firm, the management has just reason to feel elated, but if they are out, it would be a good idea to find out why. No business will make permanent headway if it lets the old customers slide while it is taking on new ones. That is one kind of turnover to be avoided at all costs.

One of the best assets of a business house is a good correspondent. The letter written in behalf of the house impresses the customer as having a great deal more authority than the spoken word of *any* employe.

A slip in courtesy, a misstatement, or a lack of interest on the part of the correspondent is nearly always fatal to an account. The customers regard a letter coming from the house as authoritative; whereas they might be disposed to overlook an error on the part of a salesman, or a floor walker, or a service man. The letter, bearing the signature of the house is seldom excused as a human failing.

In these days of stress for volume of accomplishment the business executive very frequently overlooks the need for character in the makeup of the man who writes the letters for the house. The executive is interested in the man who can reply to so many letters per hour, and forgets that when letters are replied to with this speed, they cannot possibly contain the personal interest, the sympathetic understanding, and the careful attention to the psychological result that there should be in every letter aimed to produce good feeling between customers and business organizations.

When an order has been received by mail, a well worded letter of acknowledgment is an act which shows the appreciation of the house for the order received. Many firms insist that all orders be acknowledged by a good letter.

When goods have been ordered which cannot be delivered immediately, the customer should be at once advised as to the cause of the delay. When a mistake has been made in filling an order, a letter should immediately go forward, acknowledging the error, and making arrangements to remedy it. When an order is received and it is necessary to substitute for it in whole or in part, a letter to this effect should be dispatched.

These instances indicate the need for thoughtfulness on the part of the correspondent, and they show just a few of the general functions of a correspondent which are so many times entirely overlooked in any business.

Statistics show why Customers get away from Business Houses

The mortality in the list of customers of most business houses is astonishingly large — far larger than it ought to be. In the average retail business at least fifteen per cent of the people who buy from one house this year will, for some reason or other, be purchasing from a competitor next year.

No matter what business is engaged in, a check should be kept on the active and inactive lists of customers, made up from ledger records for two or three years back.

Nearly all business men realize that customers do get away from them, but very few have made an attempt to analyze the reasons for losing customers, or to systematically investigate the facts and devise a suitable remedy.

But here is what one big retail specialty house found in checking back their sales record for eighteen months and compiling a list of active and inactive accounts.

Out of a total of 2800 customers' names, they found 300 inactive. A carefully prepared letter was sent to each name, making inquiry as to why they had discontinued buying. This letter was signed by the president of the firm, and a self addressed, stamped envelope was enclosed.

One hundred ninety-six replies were received. They were tabulated, and the answers classified in order as follows:

    47   Indifference of salesmen
    44   Attempts at substitution
    18   Errors
    18   Tricky methods
    17   Slow deliveries
    16   Over insistence of salesmen

13   Unnecessary delays in service
11   Tactless business policies
 9   Bad arrangement of store
 6   Refusal to exchange purchases
 1   Poor quality of goods

Only one answer from the entire three hundred people addressed had any fault to find with the merchandise. All the others had discontinued their purchasing because of dissatisfaction with service.

This was a decided revelation to the house and a plan was inaugurated at once to maintain as a permanent policy, a careful follow-up on all inactive accounts. This quickly checked up on delinquencies and adjusted complaints speedily, so that the customers were retained as a profitable asset for the house.

Mistakes and dissatisfaction are bound to occur just as long as we have to deal with the human element in business. The figures pointed out above, however, show that the store itself is to blame for the larger percentage of the mortality in business. The forty-seven who replied that their reason for discontinuing business was the indifference of salesmen, show that any house which is indifferent to the needs of its customers will very quickly lose their trade.

Show that you are interested in the needs of your customers, and they will show themselves interested in your store or your factory. That is the natural law of human reaction which is just as true in business as in any other field of endeavor.

The Value of a Customer

No level-headed business man will stand idly by and watch his one-time customers, whom he has learned to regard as friends, pass his store and go on to that of his competitor.

Customers are too valuable to be regarded with indifference and to be permitted to drift away. Yet we find that, even in the best of retail stores or manufacturing plants, people are allowed to do this very thing. They have been trading at a store or buying the manufacturer's goods for many years, and then without excuse, their patronage ceases, and no effort is made to re-establish their account on the ledger.

Some time ago, when I was connected with

Marshall Field & Company's retail store, we became concerned about the list of inactive accounts. Naturally, in a store of that kind there are very many of them. Some represented business of $5000 a year or more that we were not getting.

To all intents and purposes, these people had moved out of town, or passed out of life, for they no longer bought at our store. We determined at least to find out why, and a series of follow-up letters were written to each account courteously asking where we had gone amiss, and offering to right any wrong.

One account, in which we were particularly interested, was that of the wife of a large manufacturer, whose purchases represented at least $3000 a year. No reply came to our first letter, so a second was sent. It met the same fate. The third letter was written, and this too, was unanswered.

One day I visited the husband's office, sent in my card, and was told to wait: I waited for nearly an hour but finally I got an interview. When I asked him why Mrs. Blank no longer came to our store he said: " You know very well why she stopped. She had ample reason." My assurances that we did not know of the reason must have convinced him, for finally he told me the story of the break in business relations, and this is what occurred.

Mrs. Blank came into the store and ordered a $250 gown, specifying that it must be altered and delivered to her home by 6 P.M. Just as the closing bell sounded, the alteration room 'phoned the credit department to ask if it were O. K. to send out Mrs. Blank's dress on a charge.

The regular clerk had left, and the " green " hand who consulted the credit files, found no account for Mrs. Blank, and said the gown would have to go c. o. d. When the messenger took it to the Blank residence, the maid called: " Mrs. Blank, here is a c. o. d. from Field's."

Imagine the woman's surprise: She insisted it was a mistake, but the messenger was adamant. Mr. Blank was called. To settle the matter, he wrote out a check for $250.00. This was refused by the messenger, who explained that he could not accept checks.

After some difficulty and some delay, the $250 was gathered together and the gown was secured. The Blanks arrived at the dinner party, to which they were invited, nearly an hour late.

That's why the store lost $3000 a year in business from one particular customer. The error was traced through, profound apologies offered, and the account restored. Now what was the value of that customer to Marshall Field & Company? In the years that followed $30,000 was spent in the store.

Was it worth while to institute the follow-up campaign to find out the reason for dissatisfaction? The entire cost of the investigation did not exceed $20.00. Could any account of a similar amount be secured at so little cost?

It is most remarkable, however, that very few business men stop to look at the value of a customer in this light. They value any transaction solely on the profits made from one particular deal.

This shortsighted attitude is evidenced in an instance, which was uncovered by a series of follow-up letters.

A customer placed an order with the decorating department of a department store for thirteen rolls of paper to decorate a room, and engaged the services of the paper-hanger to complete the work. The paper was delivered and the work started.

Telephone calls asking to be supplied with an extra roll of paper met with the response: " Our wagons do not make deliveries out that way until next Thursday." The paper hanger left, promising to return on the following Thursday, when the balance of the paper was delivered.

For the next three days the house was in a condition of disorder and when the paper arrived no paper-hanger put in an appearance. A telephone request to the store failed to produce results, and the following Monday another paper-hanger was engaged to finish the job.

This matter was brought to the attention of the general manager of the department whose comment was: " Oh, the profit on the whole job is less than it would cost us to send a man out there specially to complete the work."

How many department managers have you who take this attitude toward a customer, and regard his value as being merely the " profit on this job." The actual results in this case were, that this customer, who had been in the habit of spending $100.00 per year with the store, discontinued his trade altogether. In the ten years which elapsed, before reconciliation was made, over $1000 in sales was lost.

These indications show the real value of a customer in a store, and point to the sound economic reason for the establishment of a mail sales promotion department which will keep customers satisfied, and induce them to continue patronage and increase goodwill influence.

How Claim Adjustments are Handled so as to Produce New Business

One of the ticklish points in any business, and one that necessitates adroit handling, is the complaint on the part of the customer.

The attitude of most business men toward a complaint is entirely wrong. They resent the complaint and take an argumentative or an injured attitude which is entirely lacking in strategy and good business sense.

Every business man who receives a complaint letter, ought to be intensely pleased because it gives him an opportunity to avoid the loss of a customer who has been trading at his store for some time. The customer who does not write but who feels dissatisfied and quits buying because of ill treatment is the one who is doing you more harm than the one who writes in and frankly tells you where your service is weak.

Not only is the complaint letter your means of saving the present customer, but it is your means of remedying conditions in your place of business which are not right, and so avoiding repetition of mistakes which might injure or destroy other customers.

If you are prepared to make an adjustment, or to give any concession to the one who is making complaint, let this be stated freely, openly, and cordially, right in the beginning of your letter. The concession which is given grudgingly, or with an apparent lack of enthusiasm may not promote goodwill.

So welcome the complaint letter as a real business opportunity, and then treat it in a businesslike way.

On your attitude toward the complaint will depend the satisfaction of customers, and their continued relations with your establishment.

If you begin your letter with a refusal of the request, a denial of the charges, or an intimation that the customer is taking an unfair advantage, you are almost sure to sever business relations.

I shall not attempt to give illustrations of the types of letters which might be considered poor, nor to suggest the types of letters which I would consider good in adjusting claims because we find that in nearly every instance, the nature of the claim is so different as to make any individual letter useful only to a very limited class.

I do, however, want to make this statement, that the finest types I have ever seen of claim adjustment letters are those which have carried with them so much confidence that not only has the customer been thoroughly satisfied, but the letter has sold new articles of merchandise.

For instance, in the case of the woman who wrote in to Sears, Roebuck and Company, complaining about a stove which she had bought. The claim adjuster at once diagnosed the case, and showed her that the trouble came from the simple fact that she had failed to open the damper regulator. Then after assuring her of the fine results she would get when she made this simple adjustment, he pointed out the value of some kitchen utensils that she could use with the stove.

He quoted prices, gave dimensions, and inclosed a circular illustrating the articles. In a little while he received a letter from the woman stating that she had done as instructed and that the stove worked well, moreover she enclosed an order for the full set of the kitchen utensils mentioned.

That man was a real mail salesman. He saw further than the immediate claim. He placed himself in the position of the person purchasing the stove and as soon as he did that, he saw not only an opportunity to adjust the claim satisfactorily, but to open up a new field of business.

New Customers, Killed by the Credit Department, can be Restored to Life

Of all of the crimes committed in the name of business, possibly more are committed by the credit and collection department than by any other branch of the business.

If there is any particular class of men who

need educating up to the value of good letters, it is the men in the collection department.

A collection man who sees only the necessity of collecting every dollar as quickly as possible, and who has no sympathetic appreciation of the other fellow's difficulties can kill more accounts in a week than a sales department can build up in six months.

For instance, the man who holds a high position in a large wholesale house in Chicago, the treasurer of the company, wrote the following letter to a customer.

" Dear Sir:

The order placed with our Mr. J. B. Brown on Monday, has been held up because your June account is unpaid. You should make it your business policy to pay up your accounts before ordering new goods."

This letter was written to a man who had been buying goods from the house for seven years, and whose account had remained unpaid because he had been away on a vacation. Is it any wonder that in the following mail, this answer was received:

" Referring to yours of the 16th, cancel the order given to your Mr. J. B. Brown, and instruct him not to call on us any more."

I could quote hundreds of instances where similar letters have been written which absolutely wreck the opportunities for business which institutions have built up at much expense and after much hard effort on the part of the sales department.

In one instance, the sales department had been after an account for two years. They had sent salesmen to call on the prospect repeatedly, and the name on the advertising list had received mailing pieces at frequent intervals.

At last an order was received.

Altogether the sales department had spent about $250 to secure this order, and when it came in it was for a trial amount — about $1000 — far less than what might be expected in the future if business relations proved satisfactory.

The habit of the company ordering was to pay all of its bills on the 15th. The credit department of the concern making the sale never informed themselves in regard to this fact. Consequently on the following month, when the salesman brought in an order for approximately $8000, the credit department noticed that the first order had not been paid, and promptly stopped shipment on the larger order. As a result the customer refused to give the salesman any further business the next time he called.

Confronted by a number of instances of this kind, the sales manager sought the assistance of the advertising manager and the correspondent on how to restore accounts killed in this way.

A consultation with the general manager showed how very necessary it was to first of all remove the cause of the mortality, and introduce into the credit department a human understanding of customers' requirements; so that full investigation of credit matters would be made, and that no interference with other departments would be undertaken by the credit manager without consultation with the department heads.

With this new policy established, the correspondents were immediately set to work on a number of accounts which had been sacrificed as a result of credit interference, and with letters breathing the spirit of coöperation and helpfulness, thirty-two per cent of the old accounts were restored.

The attitude of a well organized credit department in handling matters of this kind is best illustrated by the way in which the credit manager at the wholesale house of Marshall Field & Company took hold of the situation.

Several merchants who had been buying from the wholesale department of Marshall Field & Company had been " past due " in sending in their remittances. Instead of sending a peremptory demand for immediate payment, Mr. Higginbottom took the human view, and wrote to these merchants in a spirit of helpfulness, stating that he appreciated their position and that he knew failure to pay must be due either to a falling off in business, or to slow collections.

He offered the services of Marshall Field & Company in helping them to arrange for sales which would bring in immediate cash, or to show them methods which would result in more immediate collections.

The result of these letters was that out of seventy-two merchants written to, five paid up immediately, thirty-two wrote asking counsel on money-making sales, and thirty-three wrote for advice regarding collections.

In less than ninety days, fifty-nine of these seventy-two delinquent accounts had adopted the suggestions sent out and as a result had paid up their bills.

Every business man should remember that the house he is dealing with is human, and that the dealer will be a more substantial patron of his goods if he can help the dealer to greater success. The spirit of helpfulness is far better than a spirit of advice, or a spirit of authority.

The same thing is frequently true in regard to customers buying from retail stores. Situations arise in the individual home which means financial stress. Sometimes the advice of a good business head can restore the finances of a home so that all accounts can be taken care of promptly, for financial matters are largely a matter of management

Avoiding Customer Indifference

At least seventy per cent of the purchasing public buys in a haphazard manner. They do not care particularly for any store, or its merchandise.

The same thing can also be said of dealers who have no particular preference for any wholesale house, or any particular brand of manufactured goods.

That is because they have never been sold on the service which the organization gives. Unless they have been told in a very personal way about the excellent features offered, unless they have been informed regarding the measures provided for their benefit, they will just as readily buy from competitors.

The work of a department for merchandising by mail is to overcome customer indifference and to establish preference for a concern's merchandise, and for the service which it has to offer.

This accounts largely for the success of businesses which issue house organs, or similar monthly mailings, or who make it a practice to send out, at regular intervals, highly personalized letters.

The bulletin which is issued merely as a perfunctory affair, as something which has to be written on the first of the month, will not accomplish these results. But where human interest has been put into a story, and told frequently to those who need the particular merchandise which a concern manufactures, the results will be immediately apparent in increased sales.

CHAPTER XV

PLACE OF MAIL SELLING IN MERCHANDISING

Probably the growth of popularity of direct mail advertising is the most striking illustration of evolution we have in modern business. Only twenty years ago direct advertising was little appreciated and a neglected form of advertising. It was looked upon with indifference — even contempt.

However, ten years ago, the possibilities of using the mails to make sales began to gain recognition by business houses ' generally. With the war, and the need of direct advertising to take the place of salesmen and do its part in the great campaign of propaganda, education, and organization, the value of direct advertising demonstrated itself to the country.

The thoughts of American business men are turning more and more to the solution of the problem of economic distribution. The material growth of America will not be solved by any " back to the land " movement, or back to anything from which we have come, but it will be solved by a forward movement, a movement that speaks of greater possibilities from a smaller expenditure of energy.

The manufacturing problem — that of economic production — has, according to nearly all observers, reached its zenith in such plants as the Ford factory at Detroit, while the problem of economic distribution is just beginning to be understood.

Few advertisers realize the possibilities for development of direct mail advertising in their lines of business. When John H. Patterson placed the cash register on the market, its future was considered limited. Today it is used in every kind of retail store.

When the Addressograph was placed on the market, it was felt that there was a maximum market of eleven lines of business who were prospects. Today 200 lines of business are using Addressographs.

When the Bowser Liquid Pump was first placed on the market in the 80's the only field for sale which Mr. Bowser and his associates felt existed was in grocery stores where they recognized there was a great need for some

device for pumping oil. Today the liquid
pump is used in pumping millions of gallons
of gasoline a year as well as for pumping
scores for other liquids.

The principle of the possibilities of development of an idea should never be lost
sight of. Evolution is one of the greatest
forces in the world. It is one of the few things
that were here when the world was formed
and will always be here. It applies to direct
advertising just as it does to everything else.

Just as the mail order houses of Sears,
Roebuck & Company and Montgomery Ward
& Company started out selling small articles
thirty five years ago, and with the development of the field, added larger and larger
factors, (until they have found it possible to
sell garages, houses, furnaces, and similar
things undreamed of a few years ago), just so
the public is awakening to the fact that the
principles of selling are the same for every
commodity and that merchandising by mail
can be applied to all marketing problems.

Who Can Use Mail Selling Methods

It would be a fine thing if the salesmen for
every manufacturer or wholesaler could go in-

to towns where someone has sorted out all the
live prospects and placed a chalk mark on the
door of every man worth calling on.

Just think of the valuable time a salesman
would save if all he had to do was follow chalk
marks. No time would be wasted in missionary work, or in calls on the " impossible."
Nothing to do but step right in and start telling a sales story to a man all primed and ready
to listen. This is not an idle dream.

The right kind of direct mail sales promotion can " chalk mark " a city, a county or a
territory, at a comparatively low cost.

Direct mail advertising will find the man
who is ready to buy now. It will separate the
folks who want to talk business from the mass
of possible purchasers. It will bring inquiries
from the interested ones, inviting a salesman
to call and talk terms. It will surely and
steadily sell the products or service for any
business to those prospects who are not quite
ready to buy just now. And it will keep them
sold until such time as they are actually in
position to place an order.

Practically every type of business, regard-
less of whether it is selling merchandise or
selling service, can use mail selling methods.

Anything that can be sold, can be sold by mail or the process of making the sale influenced by mail.

One might think that the field of merchandising by mail has been fairly well exploited because merchandising by mail has been made use of by practically every activity in the United States, selling from manufacturer to consumer, wholesaler to dealer, manufacturer to jobber, manufacturer to chain stores, manufacturer to department stores, dealer to consumer, agent to purchaser, manufacturer to agent.

All of these phases of merchandising have been successfully covered in the practical selling by mail which has already been done by American manufacturers, wholesalers and retailers.

But when we say that it has been accomplished by these different types of people, we have to admit that only a small percentage of each class are making use of these selling methods, and of even this small percentage very few are handling their mail selling methods in a scientific way. Even these few who are handling their mail selling methods in an intelligent manner have not reached the limit of their sales efficiency in this field.

One of the greatest advantages of direct advertising is that it is equally available for every advertiser — large or small. It gives the small advertiser the same weapons that the large advertiser uses, and their efficiency is not diminished because they are fitted to his requirements and means.

Manufacturers find direct mail advertising a practical sales promotional aid in almost every department of business. It can be used in getting leads, building goodwill, making sales, as supplementary advertising to pave the way for salesmen to follow up inquiries, to obtain requests for catalogs, to put forth educational information and propaganda.

Public service companies have used but very little direct mail work compared to what they might use with great profit. If the public were educated as to the high ideals of most public service companies, by a consistent campaign of direct mail pieces, there would be less misunderstanding, less friction and less political interference with the operation of these very necessary parts of our social fabric.

With the growth of business associations,

the use of mail selling methods by the smaller retailer will be made possible to an increasing extent because quantity production of advertising material, when distributed among hundreds of dealers, come well within the range of their pocketbooks, whereas when each individual attempts to produce his own advertising matter for mail merchandising purposes, the cost is prohibitive.

Indications are that the use of mail merchandising methods will be extended to an increasing number of every type of business in this country, and that methods will be worked out which will enable every business house, even those of the very smallest proportions, to add this factor of sales to their merchandising plans.

Raising Funds For Churches, Schools and Charitable Institutions

In recent years, churches have been placed more on a business basis and have profited thereby, but only in very exceptional cases has the church made use of the direct mail method to increase its membership, to raise funds, or to give publicity to its activities.

Where these methods have been employed, however, the results have been astounding.

Following the late war, the drives by the various denominations for special funds to carry out a world program were largely aided by direct mail methods. Among the most noticeable of these was the Centenary Campaign of the Methodist Church which set out to raise $100,000,000 and actually raised $107,000,000 in subscriptions in a remarkably short period of time. One of the features of this campaign was the use of the minute men, and each minute man was kept in touch with the home office through direct mail methods.

Every pastor was kept in touch with the progress of the drive by the same method, and the advertising pieces distributed through the mail formed one of the features of the campaign.

Individual churches have used direct mail methods to revive their membership, bring new people to church, to raise funds for a special purpose, to inaugurate new departments, and to increase the attendance at many of their activities.

One of the most remarkable developments in the use of direct mail has, however, been by the charitable institutions. One time it was thought that money could not be raised for charity without personal solicitation, but the experience of some of the largest charity organizations has proved the fallacy of this idea, for many campaigns are carried on to thousands of people without a single individual call, but funds are raised, even in large amounts, by appeals sent out through the mails.

The United Charities of Chicago raise the greater part of their funds in this way because they give care to the preparation of the letters and other literature which they send out. Usually a simple letter is sufficient to produce results from a well selected list. Great care is taken in the preparation of this letter. Sometimes tests are made which show the pulling power of various letters before the final one is decided on.

One of the most successful campaigns ever instituted was in behalf of a college which used direct methods to get in touch with all of their alumnae, for a special drive to raise a commercial fund. The appeal from Alma Mater, coming through the mail, was responded to very generously because the campaign had been prepared right, and it produced reasons for giving which were well nigh irresistible.

Service is easy to sell by mail. Perhaps the the most popular way of merchandising service is the personalized letter sent out on representative stationery, filled-in with the name and address of the recipient, and carrying the pen-written signature of the person offering the service.

Numerous instances of substantial success in selling service by mail point to the increasing use and effectiveness of this method of soliciting clients by service organizations.

Introducing New Inventions

It is safe to say that in the merchandising of the future, the use of the mails will play an important part in introducing new inventions to the public.

In the early history of manufacture in this country, a man with an invention to market was practically limited to one or two outlets for his distribution.

The evolution of business, however, has changed this situation so that instead of having one manufacturer of an article who could make his own terms with the inventor, there are usually enough manufacturers to make competition for the article itself.

The man who has a new invention for a pump, for instance, finds that there are 724 pump manufacturers. If his invention runs along musical lines, he finds there are 600 musical instrument manufacturers.

The inventor can place his proposition before a large number of men who are in competition with each other for new ideas, and it is very likely he will obtain the right sort of proposition from some of them because he has hundreds of chances of getting a square deal whereas he formerly had only a few.

After negotiations have been made between the manufacturer and inventor, it is obvious that the object of the manufacturer would be to let every sales organization know immediately about the new invention — the improvement in his line. And here direct mail is used again and the merchandising methods which make use of the mails will quickly introduce the new invention through the retailer to the general public.

Statistics As A Guide To Sales Plan

The merchandising of the future will be guided more and more by statistics, and as the science of marketing by mail develops, statistics will be more readily available as to the results of various selling appeals. The collation of these statistics and the placing of them in readily available form, is one of the tasks that the direct mail industry should set itself at with real determination.

The information should consist of actual accomplishments in the merchandising field, with samples of the pieces which have produced sales. Accurate records of costs and results should be kept. Technical data as to number of mailings to send, kind of list, postage, style of mailing, etc., should be accumulated.

Some advertising service houses have a valuable library of practical accomplishments in the direct mail field. The advertising pieces and their records are documents filled with human and scientific interest. A prospective merchant will find it profitable to make use of this library because of the dollars that it will save him in the planning of his own campaigns.

Through this accumulated experience and data, the advertiser can check up ahead of time, and estimate the volume of sales that can be expected on any given article, plan a campaign along scientific lines, carry it out correctly in its every detail. That is the only way we know of for providing service to merchandisers which will enable them to make the best use of direct mail methods.

As each new problem is approached it becomes a little easier to handle because the results of past tests are known, and comparison with allied problems gives a fairly accurate guide as to the probable results of each new campaign.

For instance if a two-color broadside sent out to 8,000 dealers, advertising a line of shoes running from $3.00 to $8.00 retail price, sold a volume of $9,000 in shoes, it might reasonably be expected that an appropriate mailing piece sent out to a list of dealers on shirts selling from $1.50 to $3.00, would produce a volume of business satisfactory to the shirt manufacturer.

A great deal of attention has been focused

in recent years on the export field, and plans for creating business outside of the borders of this country.

When one reflects that in the United States there are at best about 112,000,000 people out of a total world population of 2,000,000,-000, the possibilities of the export field look very inviting. Of course, the purchasing power of a great many people in foreign countries is limited, but generally speaking, the standard of living throughout the world is improving from year to year, and the opportunities in the export field are becoming increasingly better.

In looking, therefore, to the development of merchandising on the part of the American manufacturer, a great deal of attention should be given to the export field and here, as nowhere else, merchandising by mail finds one of its biggest opportunities.

Consider for a moment the facts given in the earlier chapters as reasons for the development of direct mail: The high cost of transportation over long distances, the infrequency of the visits of the personal salesmen who have to travel long distances, the high cost of the selling expense occasioned by the expenses of the personal salesman. This is multiplied in the case of these salesmen introducing merchandise to a foreign country. On the other hand, merchandise introduced into a foreign country by mail is sold without any comparative increase in cost other than the postage rate. The cost of translation into foreign languages does not greatly increase the cost of the production.

The returns which many manufacturers have found from their export selling by mail have been so eminently satisfactory that they are increasing their direct mail appropriation.

This particularly applies to the Mexican and South American trade which is quick to respond to mail merchandising methods.

One well known manufacturer of cosmetics tried a Spanish folder a few years ago and whereas results of the folder in English sent to the trade in the United States had been producing only about 3 per cent of replies, the folder in Spanish sent to Mexico, Brazil and Argentine produced over 14 per cent of replies and resulted in a volume of business more than double what the English folder had produced.

Sales Inventories And What They Show

Many merchants have formed the habit of making a merchandise inventory once every year, but the number of people who make sales inventories is limited.

A sales inventory is the listing of all possible avenues for making sales, together with their probable volume, along certain advocated methods. A thorough sales inventory would show the volume of goods which could be sold through present dealers when helped by intensive campaigns to the dealers, the volume of goods that could be sold by jobber cooperation, the volume of goods that could be sold through the export field, the volume of goods that could be sold through agents, the volume of goods that could be sold by mail order methods.

With a scientifically prepared chart, showing an actual sales inventory, based on sound economics, the merchant of the future will be able to plan his marketing campaign more skillfully than the merchant of today, and when this is done, when sales are planned on this scientific basis, then the place of merchandising by mail will become an even more important factor than it is at the present time.

The opportunities for developing business and sales influence through direct mail methods are increasingly attractive. They are here now — all around us. This sales influence is gradually making itself felt in a way which will count in competition against the unprogressive firm which clings to the old ways. Merchandising by mail is giving a real advantage to the firm which systematically makes use of it.